Mysterious Visitors

The Sky People
Men Among Mankind
Forgotten Heritage
The Flying Saucer Story
Operation Earth

Mysterious Visitors

THE UFO STORY

Brinsley Le Poer Trench

STEIN AND DAY/*Publishers*/New York

First published in the United States by Stein and Day/*Publishers,* 1973
Copyright © 1971 by Brinsley Le Poer Trench
Library of Congress Catalog Card No. 72–96748
All rights reserved
Printed in the United States of America
Stein and Day/*Publishers*/ 7 East 48 Street, New York, N.Y. 10017
ISBN 0–8128–1535–1

THIRD PRINTING, 1974

TO WAVENEY

This book was originally called *The Eternal Subject* in memory of Waveney Girvan, a man who did so much to bring it into the open. He used to refer to the UFOs as "the eternal subject" when discussing them with his friends.

Waveney Girvan was the real founder of the world's leading and most respected UFO magazine, *Flying Saucer Review,* back in 1954, and ably edited it from the autumn of 1959 until he left this world in the autumn of 1964.

Waveney possessed a remarkable mind and was blessed with much wit and charm. He was held in great respect and regard by all who came into contact with him.

CONTENTS

Introduction   11

PART ONE
A Well-kept Secret

1 The Myth That Will Not Die   15
2 Mystery on the Moon   18
3 UFO Bases on Earth   22
4 The Cover-up   27

FIRST INTERLUDE

5 Saucers in the Bible   33

PART TWO
UFOs and the Psychic

6 The Paranormal Aspect   49
7 Teleportation and Cloud UFOs   50
8 Levitation and UFOs   59
9 Materialization and UFOs   65

10 Precipitations and UFOs   69
11 Expansion and Contraction of UFOs   73
12 Animals and UFOs   77
13 Telepathy and UFOs   85
14 The "Windows" and UFOs   89
15 Further Thoughts on the Paranormal   93

PART THREE

Wheels Within Wheels

16 The Mystery Airships   97
17 The Mystery Airplanes   103
18 The Mystery Rockets   107
19 The Mystery Progression   110
20 The Mystery of the Faceless Woman   114
21 The Mystery of the UFO Emblem   120

SECOND INTERLUDE

22 What Is It All About?   131

PART FOUR

A Cosmic Concept

23 The Manufacture of the Microcosm   137
24 The Manufacture of Humanity   144
25 Are We a Hybrid Race?   148
26 History Repeats Itself   153

PART FIVE

The Tremendous Tomorrow

27   The New Race   157
28   The Lattice   163
29   The Instantaneous Way to the Stars   166
30   Time Is Short   172

     Appendix A. Descriptions of UFO Shapes   176
     Appendix B. Contact   181
     Notes   184
     Index   189

(Plates 1–11 follow page 39 and Plates 12–18 follow page 124.)

ACKNOWLEDGMENTS

I wish to thank both Mr. Charles Bowen, the editor of *Flying Saucer Review,* and Mr. Gordon W. Creighton, that indefatigable consultant and contributor to the magazine, for their kind permission to quote extensively; Captain Ivar Mackay, chairman of the British UFO Research Association, for reading part of the manuscript and for his greatly valued comments and suggestions; Kiril Terziev for supplying photographs of his wonderful interpretive drawings of biblical events; the Reverend Dr. Norman Cockburn for valuable biblical research; Señor Antonio Ribera for the remarkable photographs of the UFO with the enigmatic marking; Mr. J. B. Delair, editor of the *UFO Register,* for permission to include the descriptions of UFO types in Appendix A.

Introduction

This book is a serious attempt to present a possible solution of the UFO enigma, and to come to grips with some of the mysteries surrounding the subject.

We will start by probing into the mystery of why the reality of the flying saucers is such a well-kept secret. This is almost as fascinating a puzzle as the unidentified flying objects (UFOs) themselves.

Then follows a good long hard look at the possible paranormal connection with UFOs. Some classic sightings that are probably already familiar to many students of the subject are included in the chapters on that particular aspect. These are used to indicate certain paranormal features and I hope ufologists will find this new look at them worthwhile. There is, of course, a considerable amount of new material as well.

Over ten years ago in my first book, *The Sky People,* and four years later, in my third one, *Forgotten Heritage,* I postulated that the occupants of these celestial chariots originated from other space-time continuums than our own, that is, from invisible universes. Although my books were widely read, I was regarded by many leading UFO researchers during that period as "off-beat," even to them. I was before my time.

Today, the situation is reversed. Leading ufologists such as the well-known biologist Ivan T. Sanderson; the prominent American writer John A. Keel; the editor of *Flying Saucer Review,* Charles Bowen, and the president of the British UFO

Research Association (BUFORA), Gordon W. Creighton, recognize that some or all of the UFOs *may* emanate from other space-time continuums than our own.

Next, we examine some of the remarkable anomalies that beset the subject. The "wheels within wheels" that puzzle so many of us.

Then you will be invited to participate in a mind-stretching exercise involving a cosmic concept that will, I hope, add to your own thinking on the fascinating subject of the UFOs.

Finally, we take a look at some very strange things·happening around us today, and also use our crystal ball for a glimpse into the Tremendous Tomorrow.

The Eternal Subject—the continuing saga of the flying saucers—is now reaching a momentous stage. There are signs that we are near a *dénouement.*

There is a saying that truth is stranger than fiction. When all the facts are known about the mysterious and elusive UFOs, this statement will be more than verified.

PART ONE

A Well-kept Secret

1

The Myth That Will Not Die

The last quarter of a century has seen the emergence of a myth. We use that word because the pundits have stated in an official report that unidentified flying objects (UFOs), more popularly known as flying saucers, do not exist.

Strangely, the myth refuses to die. Since the report was published in January 1969, people have gone on seeing and reporting UFOs all over the world.

How did it all begin? That is a difficult question to answer. It would seem that unknown flying craft have always been with us. There are reports all through history of strange flying disc-, cigar-, triangle-, and star-shaped objects being seen in our skies. Many well-researched books have been published listing these sightings back to the era of the ancient Egyptians. However, there are references in the world's scriptures to what we would now term UFOs. Our own Bible contains many passages about celestial chariots and the Hindu Vedas abound with accounts of flying ships called *vimanas*.

It was just after the end of the Second World War that the UFO explosion took place. Prior to. then, sightings had been sporadic, though there had been some "flaps" in the United States in 1896–97, as well as in the United Kingdom and New Zealand in 1909.

Possibly it was a coincidence, but the fact remains that the modern intensive influx of UFOs into our air space began just after the first atomic bomb had been set off in 1945. The following year Scandinavia was visited by numerous cigar-shaped objects which were termed "ghost rockets."

In 1947 the flying saucers really got around. From then onward thousands of people were seeing them. Pilots, police officers, sailors, farmers, doctors, lawyers—people in every walk of life.

The myth was seen over North and South America, Europe, Africa, Australia, New Zealand, Japan, New Guinea, and over literally every country in the world, as well as over the polar regions. The myth has also been tracked many times on radar screens, in addition to being photographed and filmed. A strange sort of myth!

The official report mentioned earlier was issued by the University of Colorado panel of scientists headed by Dr. Edward U. Condon, a distinguished physicist. This committee was convened under contract to the U.S. Air Force to investigate the UFOs.

The committee should never have been allowed to proceed with its work after the discovery of the infamous memorandum written by the project coordinator, Mr. Robert J. Low, to another member of the proposed committee before the contract had even been signed between the University and the Air Force.

The memorandum was called "Some Thoughts, on the UFO Project" and included the following passage:

". . . . Our study would be conducted almost exclusively by non-believers who, though they couldn't possibly prove a negative result, could and probably would add an impressive body of evidence that there is no reality to the observations. *The trick would be, I think, to describe the project so that, to the public, it would appear a totally objective study but, to the scientific community, would present the image of a group of non-believers trying their best to be objective, but having an almost zero expectation of finding a saucer.* One way to do this would be to stress investigation not of the physical phenomena, but rather of the people who do the observing—

the psychology and sociology of persons and groups who report seeing UFOs. If the emphasis were put here, rather than on examination of the old question of the physical reality of the saucer, I think the scientific community would quickly get the message. . . . I'm inclined to feel at this early stage that, if we set up the thing right and take pains to get the proper people involved and have success in presenting the image we want to present to the scientific community, we could carry the job off to our benefit . . ." (Italics mine.)

The discovery of this memorandum resulted in an unholy row within the committee, and the resignations and dismissals of some of its members. The whole sordid story was published in a full-length article in *Look* magazine.[1]* Since then, it has been commented on elsewhere and the sorry tale has never been refuted.[2]

The committee should have been dissolved instantly and a completely new one formed to undertake the investigations without prejudice or bias. This was not done, and although there are some worthwhile points in it, the entire Condon Report must be regarded as tainted, invalid, and without integrity.

The damage resulting from the publication of the report is incalculable. The public has been brainwashed into accepting that the UFOs do not exist. After all, Authority has stated this through the Condon Report.[3]

However, the myth has not died. The UFOs are very real. They have gone on appearing in our skies, though, as a result of the report, newspapers in the United Kingdom and in the United States have not given them their former prominence.

*The numbers in the text refer to the notes at the end of the book.

2

Mystery on the Moon

Many of us were enthralled by that magnificent film *2001: A Space Odyssey,* made by Stanley Kubrick after the novel by Arthur C. Clarke. Viewers will recall the crystalline monolith that mysteriously appeared on the moon and other planets in the film.

This was all brought vividly to mind when the following news item appeared in the London *Daily Telegraph* on July 10, 1970.

MYSTERY OF MOON SPIRES
by our New York Staff

Photographs of the lunar surface have revealed objects that appear to have been placed there by intelligent beings, it was claimed yesterday.

Mysterious spires on the moon were said to have been revealed in pictures taken by Russia's Lunar-9 and America's Orbiter-2 spacecraft four years ago.

The claims were made in the Argosy magazine, which said the Russian and American spacecraft had photographed groups of solid objects at two widely separated locations.

"These two groups of objects are arranged in definite geometric patterns and appear to have been placed there by intelligent beings."

The photographs taken by Orbiter-2 showed what

appeared to be the shadows of eight pointed spires shaped like Cleopatra's Needle.

Mrs. Judith M. Magee, writing in the *Australian Flying Saucer Review* about these mysterious spires, states that Soviet space engineer Abramov has come forward with "a somewhat startling geometrical analysis of the arrangement of these objects, which produced a pattern known in ancient Egypt as an 'abaka.' He stated that the centres of the spires of the lunar abaka are arranged in precisely the same way as the apices of the three great pyramids."[4]

Actually, over the last few years many moving and stationary objects, as well as lights, have been seen on the moon by amateur astronomers. For example, there was the controversial "bridge on the moon" first seen by the late John J. O'Neill, former science editor of the New York *Herald Tribune*. He observed through his telescope a gigantic bridge over the Mare Crisium.[5] This was in July 1953. Astronomers everywhere ridiculed his claim. Then, a month later, the late Dr. H. P. Wilkins, well-known British lunar expert, confirmed that he had sighted the bridge, although it was not as big as O'Neill had stated. The extraordinary point about the moon bridge was that although astronomers had been looking at that very spot on the moon for years, no one had noticed it before. Now we are informed that the bridge is no longer there!

It may not be widely known that our astronauts are continually seeing UFOs on their trips in space! This has been happening for years now.

Major Robert White notched up a high-altitude record when he flew the United States X-15 high altitude rocket plane to 314,750 feet on July 17, 1962. According to *Time* magazine, Major White suddenly yelled over his radio to ground control, "There are things out there!" A big object had flown alongside his plane at 3800 miles an hour. It had then passed ahead of him.[6]

While astronaut Gordon Cooper was making his fifteenth

orbit around the earth on May 16, 1963, he informed ground control when passing over Australia that a glowing green object was approaching his spacecraft. The object was also seen by those on the ground.[7]

In an earlier book we covered the UFO sightings by astronauts to some extent, but this bit of information is worth thinking about. According to an article in *Saga* magazine, Dr. Garry Henderson, a top space research scientist with General Dynamics, has stated that *all* American astronauts have seen UFOs, but have been told not to discuss their sightings with *anyone!*[8]

The general public may not realize it, but conversation can be censored out of the transmission between astronauts and ground control by the delayed-tape technique which allows a lag of up to two or three minutes between Mission Control at Houston and the continuing broadcast into your home.

Actually, amateur radio operators, "hams," who operate on different frequencies, can pick up these censored pieces of dialogue.

In this connection, there is a story going the rounds, concerning the Apollo 11 team, that Neil Armstrong and Buzz Aldrin saw something very spectacular on the moon, that their conversation about this was deleted from the live broadcast by the delayed-tape technique just mentioned, and that some radio hams picked this up. It is, of course, possible that this did occur, in view of all the other true incidents that have been related; perhaps if any radio hams did hear anything unusual they will fill me in.[9]

However, it would seem that UFOs accompanied Apollo 12 part of the way to the moon. Here is a quotation from *Saga* magazine:

"On Friday evening, November 14, 1969, observatories all over Europe sighted two bright flashing unknowns near the path of Apollo 12 which was on its way to putting America's second team of astronauts on the moon.

"Seen through huge telescopes one object appeared to be

following the spacecraft, and one seemed to be moving in front of it. Both objects were blinking on and off rapidly! On Saturday, November 15th, our three astronauts: Pete Conrad, Dick Gordon and Allan Bean, reported to Mission Control in Houston, that they had indeed spotted two bogeys 132,000 miles out. Why doesn't NASA tell us the whole story behind Apollo 12's mysterious encounter with flying saucers?"[10]

One reassuring fact is that though so many astronauts have seen UFOs in space, there have been no hostile incidents out there.

Even though America has now landed three teams of astronauts on the moon and brought them back safely, there is still a great deal to be explained. There are too many question marks sticking out like a sore thumb. Why does not NASA come clean about the large number of UFOs seen by astronauts? Is the moon being used as a UFO base?

What about those enigmatic "moon domes"? They were first noted nearly forty years ago. By 1960 more than two hundred had been recorded on the lunar surface. Even more oddly, it was noticed that they moved about on the moon from one position to another.

Both Dr. Walter Riedel, late director of the Peenemunde base in Germany, and the American astronomer Dr. Carl Sagan expressed the view some years ago that the UFO occupants were using the moon as a base from which to observe the earth.

There is supposed to be only a very thin atmosphere on the moon, but perhaps a very advanced race could have developed underground installations and living accommodations, and put in their own air-conditioning systems to overcome the lack of oxygen. A rather startling idea, but so would color television, radar, and our own spacecraft have been a few hundred years ago.

One day we shall know for certain. However, one thing we do know: the truth is being withheld from us.

3

UFO Bases on
Earth

In recent years there has been a tremendous amount of UFO activity over South America, especially Argentina.

In an article published in *Flying Saucer Review,* Gordon W. Creighton described a massive UFO visitation of Argentina in 1962, and wrote:

"Indeed, during the 24 hours from midnight of Saturday 12 to Sunday 13 of May, UFOs were seen all over the Argentine, and landings occurred at several places, such as Oncativo (Cordoba Province) and Zapala (Nequen). One newspaper said that this flood of sightings might well mark a new era with regard to the UFO problem, a key-day in the history of mankind. The paper added that strange cosmic happenings throughout the country had had profound emotional impact upon the many eyewitnesses. . . .

"On June 13 the Buenos Aires paper *El Mundo* reported that there had been so many saucer sightings over the Bahia Blanca area that the Chief of Police in La Plata had summoned all eyewitnesses to appear before him and give statements. Some of the reports were of landings. The paper described the events as sensational and said the UFOs were visitors from space.

"During the night of June 15, at Mar del Plata, numerous people saw a UFO, while at the neighbouring coast resort of Miramar a cigar was seen at 9:30 P.M., flying in from the direction of the South Atlantic. The whole craft was vividly illuminated and carried, in addition, three very bright lights (red in the center, yellow on the right, and green on the left). The apparent size of the cigar was greater than the diameter of the moon."[11]

Mr. Creighton went on to give a number of well-authenticated reports culled from the large quantity of newspaper clippings sent by the review's correspondents in South America. Here is another especially interesting one.

"At about 2 P.M. on July 19, the whole body of over 150 workmen at the Auto Union DKW Car Plant at Saucer Viejo (near Santa Fé, which is northwest of Buenos Aires) saw a cigar moving rapidly towards the northeast. It seemed to be at a height of about 1000 meters and gave out frequent blinding flashes. It was silent and left no trail, climbed and rapidly disappeared. Observers said the same type of craft had been seen there several times before."

The event that really caused a furor was when a UFO landed on the aerodrome at Cambá Punat (province of Corrientes, far northeast tip of Argentina).

"The airport manager, Señor Luis Harvey, explained that he had been warned by his staff that an unannounced aircraft was about to land. He ran out on to the field and saw a luminous object circling above at high speed. Failing to get any reply to their signals, he and his staff prepared for a landing, but when the object came down they were astonished to see that it was no aeroplane at all but a completely spherical body that hung, hovering and also revolving, a few feet above the same spot on the runway for some three to four minutes emitting all the while powerful blue, green, and orange flashes. Then, as the astonished officials approached, it climbed and vanished at staggering speed. The incident was at once reported to the authorities and an intensive investigation was launched.

Various newspapers carried reports and commented on this fantastic event. Creighton wrote: "La Razón (Buenos Aires) said: 'We do not believe the true explanation of these occurrences can be kept secret much longer.' *Los Andes,* a paper published in the Andean province of Mendoza, voiced the same view, and another important northern paper had the following significant comment: 'The arrival of this interplanetary craft on an aerodrome in the Province of Corrientes—a fact that can in no wise be disputed, given the manner of its appearance and the calibre of the eyewitnesses—serves to strengthen the view *that there may be Space Peoples' bases somewhere in the country, in view of the great number of recent sightings.' " (Italics mine.)

However, an even more blatant saucer landing on an airport occurred in December.

"On December 22, the Buenos Aires papers reported that, a day or so previously, a saucer had landed at 2:15 A.M. on one of the main runways of the International Airport at Ezezia, near Buenos Aires. The machine had remained there, sitting on the runway, until disturbed by the arrival of a giant Pan American DC-8 passenger plane. The principle witness interviewed by the Press was Señor Horacio Alora, officer in charge in the Flight Control Tower. He said that he and his colleague Señor José Besutti had watched as the intensely luminous UFO had landed some 2000 metres from the Control Tower. At that distance the object had the apparent size of a football. When it took off again, it went straight up to an estimated height of 500 or 600 meters, and then made off at vertiginous speed. He and his colleagues had in fact been getting ready to bring in the Pan American DC-8, and the behavior of the UFO was consequently something that they had to watch most carefully. One of the Buenos Aires newspapers pointed out, in commenting on this case, that such a landing on an important international airfield proved clearly that the saucers were no longer content to land merely in out-of-the-way places. They were now coming down boldly on the principle airfields of the country. . . ."

It can clearly be seen from the foregoing startling incidents that the UFOs were flying and landing, wherever they wished, all over Argentina in 1962. It would seem very likely that they had established bases in the more inaccessible mountaineous areas. However, at the same time as all this activity was going on, many UFOs were seen to dive into and emerge out of the sea off the coast of the country.

Creighton gives an interesting example. "In an interview with journalists which appeared in various papers in August 1962, Señor Vicente A. Bordoli, a truck driver living at Mar del Plata, stated that when driving southward along National Highway No. 3, which skirts the South Atlantic coast of the Argentine, he and his son Hugo Bordoli had frequently seen strange luminous craft both entering and leaving the sea. In his view these craft, veritable flotillas of them, *are controlled by signals emanating from underwater bases, perhaps from large submarine mother-craft.* Señor Bordoli concluded his statement by saying: *'It is absolutely certain that in the depths of the Gulf of San Matias there is a flying saucer base. . . .'* " (Italics mine.)

During 1963–64 UFO activity in South America continued, if anything, on an even wider scale, involving Peru and Brazil, as well as Argentina. This infiltration of South America has continued ever since and now, according to Spanish newspaper reports, the UFOs have a base in the depths of Lake Titicaca, which borders Peru and Bolivia, and is some twelve thousand feet up in the High Andes. People living near the lake have frequently seen saucers heading toward it and vanishing.[12]

Why so much emphasis on South America? It would seem that the continent contains many areas that are sparsely populated. In the Argentine, the land is rugged and ideal terrain for the ufonauts to establish bases. Many strange lights have been observed flitting to and fro in the mountainous regions of the High Andes.

If you think that Señor Vincente A. Bordoli's statement about underwater bases a bit "way out," then there is one scientist who would probably not agree. He is the highly respected botanist Ivan T. Sanderson. He is a former member of British Naval Intelligence, a Fellow of the Royal Society, and has taken part in many zoological expeditions around the world. One of the main themes of his notable book *Invisible Residents* is the proposition that an underwater civilization has existed, possibly for millennia, capable of space travel.[13]

Sanderson points out that the oceans occupy three quarters of the surface of our planet, and are often over two miles deep. We know almost nothing about what goes on at the bottom of the oceans, but, Sanderson states, we do know from ships' logs and from eyewitness accounts that many objects have been observed entering and leaving the seas.

It is possible, then, that the UFOs have established bases in the oceans for a very long period of time, and are now busy extending these to land ones in isolated areas, particularly in South America.

If this is the case, then surely the authorities must be aware of this significant situation. However, it is one of the many things in the UFO story that we are not officially told about. One more instance of the great cover-up.

4

The Cover-up

For the past two decades the U.S. Air Force had a project which handled all UFO reports sent in by the public. In the early days it was known as Project Sign; then as Project Grudge, and for most of the last twenty years as Project Blue Book.

The late Captain Edward J. Ruppelt, head of Blue Book from early 1951 until September 1953, after his retirement from the Air Force wrote a fine book called *The Report on Unidentified Flying Objects*. In one chapter Ruppelt stated that he had qualms as to whether the project was just a front, a cover-up for some other real investigation of the UFOs.[14]

Some years ago it became obvious to me that Blue Book was not doing a real investigation, but merely explaining away many sightings as rational objects, natural phenomena, and hoaxes.

At that time I found myself in Paris in connection with my job on an aviation magazine. I met an American who was then working in the publicity section of Republic Aviation's Paris office. During conversation over lunch it came out that he had worked on Project Blue Book. This was his last assignment before leaving the U.S. Air Force.

I asked him about his work with Blue Book. His job was fieldwork, including interviewing eyewitnesses of UFOs. He told me that their brief was to rationally explain as many sightings as possible. Many people, he told me, sincerely misrepresented what they had seen. However, there were a few sightings that they couldn't explain.

"What happened to those?" I asked.

"They were filed away," was his reply.

The sightings that could not be explained were the most important ones. Yet, a former member of Blue Book told me that they were filed away.

Since the publication of the Condon committee's report, the U.S. Air Force has used this as a convenient excuse to close down their Project Blue Book.

Now, like Ruppelt, I am sure that all these "unknowns" are being investigated by some intelligence group in the United States. It is my conviction that it always has been covertly at work.

It has now been disclosed that the Central Intelligence Agency (CIA), which has ramifications all over the world, has got involved with the UFO business.

Dr. James E. McDonald, senior physicist, Institute of Atmospheric Physics, and professor, Department of Meteorology, University of Arizona, was given permission as a scientist to look through the files of Project Blue Book after it had officially closed down. He startled ufologists by announcing that in his look through the files he came upon evidence that the CIA had initiated a program specifically to debunk the flying saucers in the early nineteen-sixties![15]

You may well ask, why? The reason given was that the U.S.A. was then involved in the Korean War and that too much concern with UFOs would take the minds of Americans off their war. Sounds a little thin to me.

There have been many cases of both CIA and FBI agents calling on members of the public who have seen UFOs.

David R. Saunders and R. Roger Harkins, in their book *UFOs? Yes!*, which is a reply to the Condon Report, have plenty to say about CIA involvement. Saunders is an ex-member of the official study group and one of those who left the committee after the discovery of the Low memorandum.

This is their assessment of the CIA involvement.

"(1) After the tragedy at Pearl Harbor our government created an organization—the CIA—designed specifically to make sure that something like Pearl Harbor never happens again.

"(2) UFO reports exist.

"(3) In the reports we find patterns which indicate that the reports are based upon real occurrences.

"(4) If UFO reports are based upon real occurrences, that is, actual physical objects invading our air space, this becomes a national security problem of prime importance—exactly the sort of thing the CIA was designed to handle.

"(5) The existence of unidentified vehicles invading our air space must be interpreted as indicating the existence of a possible unknown enemy.

"(6) Standard intelligence procedures would require that all information of this nature be withheld from the general public until firm conclusions could be reached since any disclosures might furnish aid and comfort to the unknown enemy.

"(7) This would indicate that the CIA cannot avoid the responsibility for the problem of the UFO mystery. In retrospect we can see that the Robertson Committee [a panel set up to evaluate UFO reports a number of years ago] was a device used by the CIA to establish a cover program, namely Project Blue Book, to draw attention from a covert program designed to solve the UFO mystery for intelligence purposes."[16]

That assessment by Saunders and Harkins of CIA involvement sums up the position very well. In short, until the covert military intelligence group investigating the UFO situation comes up with some pretty firm idea of the UFO mystery and of the ufonauts' intentions, then they are going to keep the whole thing under wraps. This explains the many ridiculous "explanations" put out by the authorities about UFOs sighted over the years by experienced pilots who know what there is in the sky. They have been told that what they saw was the planet Venus, spots before their eyes, and many other ludi-crous things. That is why pilots got sick of handing in UFO reports.

The part of the CIA in all this has been to try and play the whole thing down (witness Dr. McDonald's disclosure) and to ferret out anything that might be of interest to the actual, real investigation covertly in progress.

The fact is, the investigating group is aware of the reality of UFOs but does not know what to do about it. They are defeated and at a complete loss as to how to cope with the situation. The major factor confronting them is that the UFOs are paranormal, that is, from invisible universes, and their occupants are capable of using extrasensory powers. Possibly not all of them. There is some evidence to support the conten-tion that humanoid robots are being used to carry out some jobs here. The authorities just don't know how to put this all over to the public! We shall see in the next few chapters evidence supporting these statements that the UFOs may well come from other space-time continuums.

We sympathize to some extent with the authorities in their dilemma. It is also appreciated that back in 1938, when Orson Welles broadcast H. G. Wells' *War of the Worlds,* there was widespread panic. The broadcast was so realistic that many people thought the Martians were invading the world and streamed out into the streets. It took some persuading to get all those refugees with their belongings to return home again!

Obviously, the authorities don't want such a thing to hap-pen again. Surely, though, the long-term plan should have been to gradually educate the public up to the time when an announcement could be made. The public would then have been prepared for better or worse. Now, the authorities are running the risk that if a mass landing were to take place tomorrow, then a far worse panic might occur. Mark you, I don't think this likely, as it is my personal opinion that the Sky People are too wise to take such action at this moment.

Nevertheless, an informed public is a prepared public.

FIRST
INTERLUDE

5

Saucers
in the Bible

In *The Sky People* I dealt to a great extent with biblical incidents that could have a UFO connotation. For instance, what caused the walls of Jericho to fall down. I suggested that the Sky People gave the Israelites some vibrationary subsonic secret which enabled them to strike the right note when sounding the trumpets.[17]

I also mentioned the three men—angels, according to the Bible—who came to Abraham. These angels talked, ate, washed, and drank with him. I suggested that they were Sky People.

These angels told Abraham they were going to destroy the wicked city of Sodom. Abraham, you will recall, pleaded for the lives of righteous men, and the Lord agreed to his request.

Then two men visited Lot, who was sitting in the gate of Sodom. He, too, welcomed them, and bowed with his face to the ground. He, too, "made them a feast, and did bake unleavened bread, and they did eat." (Genesis 19:3)

Many more biblical incidents were described in that earlier book of mine showing that the Bible is really the greatest flying saucer book of them all, apart from its illuminating and more important spiritual content.

For instance, Moses was commanded by the Lord to bring the Israelites, who had been oppressed by Pharaoh, out of the land of Egypt. This he did and according to the Bible, the Israelites were led through the wilderness near the Red Sea.

"And the Lord went before them day by day in a *pillar of a cloud,* to lead them the way; and by night in a *pillar of fire,* to give them light; to go by day and night. He took not away the pillar of the cloud by day, nor the pillar of fire by night, from before the people." (Exodus 13:21–22; italics mine.)

The pillar of cloud by day and the pillar of fire by night, that guided and protected the Israelites, could be likened to a very accurate description of a modern UFO.

The splendidly executed interpretative drawings of biblical events illustrating this chapter are by Kiril Terziev.

Plate 1 shows Moses leading the Israelites when the Lord came down on Mount Sinai. "And the Lord came down upon Mount Sinai, on the top of the Mount: and the Lord called Moses up to the top of the Mount; and Moses went up." (Exodus 19:20)

However, the all-important clue is in the following verse! "And the Lord said unto Moses, Go down, charge the people, lest they break through unto the Lord to gaze, and many of them perish."

We certainly know that if people get too close to a UFO they can suffer injuries or even death, if the power is on.

Ezekiel's famous meeting with spacecraft is the subject of plates 2 and 3. "And I looked, and, behold, a whirlwind came out of the north, a great cloud, and a fire infolding itself, and a brightness was about it, and out of the midst thereof as the colour of amber, out of the midst of the fire." (Ezekiel 1:4)

The whole of the first chapter of Ezekiel contains probably the finest description in the Bible of a spacecraft landing and taking off. This incident took place in the land of the Chaldeans, by the river Chebar.

Very full accounts and commentaries on this event have been given by other writers. Suffice it to say here that when reading Ezekiel's own description, it is well to remember that he was not living in a mechanical age. Ezekiel had to rely on things with which he was familiar in making his report, such as birds, animals, people, and chariots with wheels. If we bear that in mind, then it will be realized that this is a wonderful UFO landing report.

Another outstanding account of a spaceship in the Old Testament is the story of Elijah being taken up in a whirlwind. It is interesting to note that both Ezekiel and the writer of the two books of *Kings* in the Bible refer to a UFO as a whirlwind.

Plate 4 shows Elisha at the ascension of Elijah. "And it came to pass, when the Lord would take up Elijah into heaven by a whirlwind, that Elijah went with Elisha from Gilgal." (II Kings 2:1)

Incidentally, there are at least two occasions on which Enoch is carried off in a whirlwind. These are described in the Book of Enoch, which is possibly the most important apocalyptic manuscript extant, apart from those in the Bible.

Once again, we can only postulate that the ancients could only describe these vehicles by calling them after something with which they were familiar. After all, modern UFOs often come like "a whirlwind out of the north." "And it came to pass, when they were gone over, that Elijah said to Elisha, Ask what I shall do for thee, before I be taken away from thee. And Elisha said, I pray thee, let a double portion of thy spirit be upon me." (II Kings 2:9)

Now this verse is very interesting as it indicates Elijah had advance information that he was to be taken up. We will be discussing, in a later section of this book, modern cases where people have been given advance knowledge of a contact with Sky People. Other instances, too, where individuals have had a sudden impulse to drop whatever they were doing, and go up a hill or to some other place, where they would see a spaceship. All this seems to point out the possibility that the Sky People use telepathic abilities in contacting earth residents.

Elijah's advance information turned out to be correct, for the Bible tells us he was taken up by a whirlwind into heaven.

Plate 5, showing horses and chariots of fire around Elisha, vividly illustrates the following verses. "And he said, Thou hast asked a hard thing: nevertheless, if thou see me when I am taken from thee, it shall be so unto thee; but if not, it shall not be so. And it came to pass, as they still went on, and talked, that, behold, there appeared a chariot of fire, and horses of fire, and parted them both asunder; and Elijah went up by a *whirlwind* into heaven." (II Kings 2:10–11; italics mine.)

The Bible states that Jacob was the son of Isaac and Rebekah, and the father of the twelve tribes of Israel. He was the twin brother of Esau. However, Esau was born first, but Jacob through a trick caused his brother to relinquish his birthright.

Nevertheless, despite this early misdemeanor, Jacob had several divine revelations or actual contacts with angels of the Lord.

For example, Plate 6, *Ma-ha-na-im and God's Host,* depicts an early contact of Jacob with divine beings.

"And Jacob went on his way, and the angels of God met him. And when Jacob saw them, he said, This is God's host: and he called the name of that place Mahanaim." (Genesis 32:1–2)

Finally, after many vicissitudes, Jacob migrated to Egypt, receiving on the way the promise that God would make of him a great nation which would come out of Egypt. This was the dream of Jacob (see plate 7). He died at the ripe old age of 147.

More than once in the Bible, we come across personages who start off their lives in the wrong way, and end up as revered and respected beings. For instance, there is Saul, who persecuted Jesus and the Christians, until he had his famous "illumination," or contact, on the road to Damascus, and subsequently, became St. Paul.

In *The Sky People,* I stated that scientists have not been able to solve the mystery of the "star" that appeared in the heavens at the time of the birth of Jesus. The star of Bethlehem. Astronomers have found that no such star should have been in the heavens at that time. "When they had heard the king, they departed; and, lo, the star, which they saw in the east, went before them, till it came and stood over where the young child was. When they saw the star, they rejoiced with exceeding great joy." (Matthew 2: 9–10)

I wrote: "Many people throughout the world who have studied the phenomenon of flying saucers hold the view that the star of Bethlehem was a gigantic spaceship. Many spaceships seen at night have appeared to witnesses as bright as the stars. Notice, too, how the 'star' went before them, till it came and stood over (hovered) where the young child was."

The star of Bethlehem which led the three kings to the Christ child is similar in some respects to the spacecraft that was a pillar of cloud by day and a pillar of fire by night, the one that led the Israelites through the wilderness.

Let us now look at the miraculous outward transformation of Christ on a high mountain with his disciples Peter, James, and John. "And after six days Jesus taketh Peter, James, and John his brother, and bringeth them up into a high mountain apart. And was transfigured before them: and his face did shine as the sun, and his raiment was white as the light. And, behold, there appeared unto them Moses and Elias talking with him." (Matthew 17: 1–3)

This wonderful scene is beautifully illustrated in Plate 8, *The Transfiguration.*

Mary the mother of Jesus, Mary Magdalene, and Mary the mother of James the Less and Joses had all been present at the crucifixion of Jesus. In the Bible it is stated that both Mary Magdalene and Mary the mother of James and Joses were present at the tomb, but we are not told specifically that Mary the mother of Jesus was there too. However, I think we can conclude that she would most certainly have been at the tomb.

Plate 9 shows *The Three Marys at the Tomb.*

"In the end of the sabbath, as it began to dawn toward the first day of the week, came Mary Magdalene and the other Mary to see the sepulchre. And, behold, there was a great earthquake: for the angel of the Lord descended from heaven, and came and rolled back the stone from the door, and sat upon it. His countenance was like lightning, and his raiment white as snow: And for fear of him the keepers did shake, and became as dead men. And the angel answered and said unto the women, Fear not ye: for I know that ye seek Jesus, which was crucified. He is not here: for he is risen, as he said. Come, see the place where the Lord lay." (Matthew 28: 1–6)

The Ascension of Jesus is illustrated in Plate 10. When you consider the way Elijah, Enoch, and other biblical people of giant spiritual stature were taken up into the skies by a "whirl-wind," it would not be altogether surprising for Jesus to leave in a similar manner. It is appreciated that this is a highly controversial suggestion, but food for celestial thought.

Finally, we come to *The Sighting of St. Peter.* Plate 11. Peter was one of the most important of the disciples, though he denied Jesus at the most crucial point. However, afterward he assumed the leadership of the early Christians and did fine missionary work. Ultimately, he, too, was crucified.

The sighting of St. Peter as given in the Bible could be interpreted as a psychic happening. On the other hand it has similarities to modern UFO phenomena.

"On the morrow, as they went on their journey, and drew nigh unto the city, Peter went up upon the housetop to pray about the sixth hour: And he became very hungry, and would have eaten: but while they made ready, he fell into a trance. And saw heaven opened, and a certain vessel descending unto him, as it had been a great sheet knit at the four corners, and let down to earth: Wherein were all manner of four-footed beasts of the earth, and wild beasts, and creeping things, and fowls of the air. And there came a voice to him, Rise, Peter, kill, and eat. But Peter said, Not so Lord; for I have never eaten any thing that is common or unclean. And the voice spake unto him again the second time, What God hath cleansed, that call not thou common. This was done thrice: and the vessel was received up again into heaven." (Acts 10:9–16)

Subsequently, Peter came to understand that the vision he

had experienced meant that people of all races and colors could become Christians.

In this chapter we have described some of the many biblical events that have a similarity to the UFO phenomena today. It would seem that the Sky People and their celestial chariots were very often in contact with our predecessors in biblical times.

Plate 1: Moses leading the Israelites when
the Lord came down on Mount Sinai

Plate 2: Ezekiel:
A whirlwind came
out of the north

Plate 3: The prophet Ezekiel, the celestial
ships, and the living beings

41

Plate 4: Elisha at the ascension of Elijah

Plate 5: Horses
and chariots
of fire
around Elisha

Plate 6: Ma-ha-na-im and God's host

Plate 7: The dream of Jacob

Plate 8: The
Transfiguration

44

Plate 9: The three Marys at the tomb

Plate 10: The
Ascension of Jesus

Plate 11: The sighting of St. Peter

PART TWO

UFOs
and the Psychic

6

The Paranormal Aspect

There is considerable evidence that the UFOs appearing in our skies have some connection with psychic phenomena. We are dealing here with a difficult problem. Both those who believe in UFO phenomena and those who believe in psychic phenomena have their respective followings, which sometimes overlap. However, neither the UFOs nor psychic phenomena have actually been officially recognized by the powers that be. So, what we are attempting to do now is to show a connection between two subjects which officially do not exist!

Some months ago, an article called "UFOs and the Occult," by Captain Ivar Mackay, chairman of the British UFO Research Association (BUFORA), was published over two successive issues of *Flying Saucer Review.*[18]

Captain Mackay listed certain apparent similarities between psychic and UFO phenomena, which seemed to show up in subjects such as teleportation, levitation, materializations, expansion and contraction of objects, and many others.

We must make it clear that though Captain Mackay listed these similarities, he did not state that psychic or occult phenomena were identical to UFO phenomena. He was merely pointing to the possible connections.

In these next few chapters we will take some of the items Captain Mackay has listed and give examples of an apparent connection with UFO phenomena. I think this is the first serious attempt to make such a comparison in such depth, and hope that it will be of use to other workers in the combined fields.

7

Teleportation and UFOs

My various dictionaries do not give a definition of teleportation. They all give one for telepathy. I think that telepathy has now gained a certain recognition in the scientific world. It is well known that this is being used in the military sphere, as we shall see later.

Mr. R. Tambling, in his book *Flying Saucers—Where They Come From,* gives his definition of teleportation as "a word coined to express the idea of the transmission of matter from one point to another without physical connection." That seems to express the meaning pretty well.[19]

We will commence our introduction to teleportation by giving you a story almost four centuries old. It may or may not have anything to do with UFOs, but it is, none the less, extremely fascinating. The tale is also interesting because the central figure landed in Mexico City after being teleported from Manila in the Philippines. As you will see later on in this chapter, so did most of the people in modern teleportation cases! Perhaps, after all, the gentleman we are going to tell you about from four centuries back could have been taken there by a UFO. It will, at least, let you know that teleportation is not something that applies only to our day and age. Let us, therefore, give the stage over to Gordon Creighton and enjoy his most interesting account taken from *Flying Saucer Review.*[20]

"On the morning of October 25, 1593, a Spanish soldier suddenly appeared on the Plaza Mayor (the Principal Square) of Mexico City. He was wearing the insignia of the regiment which at that moment was guarding the walled city of Manila, in the Philippine Islands, more than 9,000 miles away on the other side of the Pacific Ocean. How did this soldier come to be in Mexico City? The truth is that he had no idea. All he knew was that he had suddenly found himself no longer in Manila, but in Mexico. But there was something else that he said he *did* know. He said that His Excellency Don Gómez Pérez Dasmarinas, Governor of the Philippines, was dead. A preposterous rumor of course. But one that spread through the Mexican capital like wildfire.

"Although puzzled as to how precisely the soldier could have traveled so far without so much as soiling his uniform, the Spanish authorities in Mexico jailed him as a deserter from the Manila garrison. An awkward Fortean 'damned fact' was thus safely swept under the carpet, and no doubt folk breathed again with relief.

"And so the weeks passed, while our soldier languished in the brig; the long slow weeks necessary for news to travel by galleon along the regular sailing route from Spain, which runs via Manila to Acapulco, the port on the west coast of Mexico. From Acapulco the news would pass by messenger up across the great sierras and into the sky-girt Valley of Mexico.

"And then suddenly Mexico City was full of the news. His Excellency Don Gómez Pérez Dasmarinas, Governor of the Philippines for King Philip II, was dead—murdered by a mutinous Chinese crew off Punta de Azufre just as he was setting sail on a military expedition against the Molucca Islands! And, moreover, he had been murdered on the very day that the mysterious soldier from the Manila garrison had appeared on the Plaza Mayor of Mexico City.

"The Most Holy Tribunal of the Inquisition, always alert for signs of witchcraft and 'diablaria,' took charge of the case. But still the soldier could not tell them how he had traveled from Manila to Mexico. All he could tell them was that it had been 'in less time than it takes a cock to crow.'

"The Inquisition ordered that the man be returned to

Manila for further investigation of the matter, and on his arrival there it was established beyond question, on the word of not a few witnesses, that the soldier had indeed been there on duty in the city of Manila on the night of October 24, 1593, just as it was proven beyond any peradventure that on the following morning he had been apprehended on the Plaza Mayor in Mexico City, over 9,000 miles away.

"There are reliable records of this episode.[21] It is no fabrication. And the best term with which we can label it, is one already familiar to us from the annals of psychic research: teleportation."

Now, many cases of teleportation have involved clouds. There are numerous instances where those taken up by cloud UFOs have not returned. The Bible gives many examples of clouds in connection with UFO phenomena which were covered in my first book. Enoch, Ezekiel, Elijah and other biblical characters come into this category.

However, we will now concentrate on times more applicable to our own. Let us first refer to a strange incident from the first World War, related by Jacques Vallée in his fascinating book *Passport to Magonia*.[22]

Very briefly, on August 28, 1915, during the final days of severe fighting at "Hill 60," Suvla Bay, during the Gallipoli campaign, in which the Australians were participating, a most extraordinary event took place.

August 28 was a beautiful clear day, but it was observed that six or eight "loaf of bread" clouds, all alike, were hovering over Hill 60. These clouds, despite a strong breeze, did not move.

A British regiment of several hundred men, the First Fourth Norfolk, was seen marching up a sunken road toward Hill 60, but one of these clouds was hovering over the road. The regiment marched into the cloud but did not come out to deploy and fight at Hill 60.

After the last file had disappeared into the cloud, it unobtrusively moved away and so did the other clouds.

In his book Vallée published a letter signed by several witnesses of the event. The regiment was posted as "missing" or "wiped out" and, according to the letter, "on Turkey surrendering in 1918, the first thing Britain demanded of Turkey was the return of this regiment. Turkey replied that she had neither captured this regiment, nor made contact with it and did not know it existed. A British regiment in 1914–18 consisted of any number between 800 and 4000 men. Those who observed this incident vouch for the fact that Turkey never captured that regiment, nor made contact with it."

This is one of the most remarkable and unexplained mysteries of modern times. Was a whole British regiment taken up by a huge UFO hovering in a cloud above the sunken road near Hill 60? If so, this must be one of the cases where those taken up in a cloud UFO have not returned.

Modern ufology teems with references to cloud cigars. The distinguished French author Aimé Michel cites many cases of cloud cigars seen over France, notably sightings at Oleron and Gaillac in 1952; Vernon in August, 1954; St.-Prouant in September 1954, and many others.

Michel stated that these reports "lend color to the idea that the 'great cloud cigar' may be a 'mother ship' to which are 'attached,' in some way that we do not understand, smaller and more mobile craft, which come and go within certain limits around the large ship. If this is so, when the big craft is seen at a certain place we should find many other observations nearby."

He then went on to describe such an event seen over Essones, St.-Fargeau, and Ponthierry, with many witnesses in these different areas. Just before 8 P.M. on the evening of Wednesday, September 22, 1954, one of them, M. Rabot, in the words of Michel, "was driving on Route N-7 toward St. Fargeau and Ponthierry (from north to south), when he noticed, above him at a seemingly high altitude—a little below the clouds—a large luminous object which he described as circular, red, and *surrounded by a sort of luminous vapor, the same color as that emanating from the object.* Here we recognize the constant feature which accompanies the 'cigar' in vertical position: it appears only in a cloud."[23]

I can vouch for the existence of this type of luminous cloud object from personal experience. One evening in November 1961, my former wife and I saw one from the kitchen of our top-floor South Kensington flat in London. My wife, who was standing by the sink before a very large old-fashioned window, suddenly called me over to her side.

The view directly out of that window is obscured by other flats, but looking slightly toward the left it is possible to see some way over the rooftops. In the distance there was a strange pinpoint of light gradually coming closer. We pulled down the top section of the window to ensure that it was no reflection. It was dark, but a clear night. The object was moving slowly, in a sort of zig-zag fashion, and appeared to be getting very close. However, at night it is very difficult to estimate distances. When it came fairly close the object changed direction toward our left. The result was that it no longer looked circular, but now became very roughly oval-shaped, and certainly more elongated. It made no sound.

The object was definitely surrounded by luminous vapor. Here, I would affirm that the description of what we saw tallied with that of M. Rabot, with the exception that our UFO was not reddish in color but a rather eerie off-white. However, Aimé Michel does state that UFOs are subject to color changes, and this has been well borne out by other people's reported sightings.

It should be added that there was some definition to be seen inside the surrounding vapor or cloudlike appearance of the UFO. It was obviously not a meteor going at that slow speed, nor did it behave like a balloon. There was no question of its being an aircraft, as no navigational lights were blinking on and off underneath it. In South Kensington you get used to aircraft passing over every few minutes on their way to London Airport.

Actually, just about half a minute after the UFO had passed from view, an airliner flew over lit up like a saloon, navigational lights blinking on and off, and making a great noise. The contrast was quite uncanny.

One other thing. After the UFO had gone my head was full

of ideas. We will be discussing the possibility that the UFO occupants can impress ideas upon people further on in our study of the paranormal aspect.

We have got a little away from teleportation. However, these cloud UFOs do have a big bearing on the connection of teleportation with ufology, as we shall see. We have already given the example of the "sugar-loaf" clouds at Hill 60.

In an earlier book we discussed in some detail the amazing case of Dr. and Mrs. Gerardo Vidal, who were driving home from a family reunion party at Chascomus in the Argentine. Suffice it to say here that they drove into a thick mist not long after leaving Chascomus and knew no more till they found themselves still in their car on a dirt road near Mexico City, some 4500 miles away. Forty-eight hours after leaving the party Dr. Vidal telephoned friends in the Argentine advising of their whereabouts. The Vidals could not account for what had happened during that elapse of time![24]

Now, here is a fascinating Japanese case involving a cloud UFO, taken from *Flying Saucer Review*.

"Shortly after 8 A.M. on November 19, 1963, a Mr. Kinoshita, acting manager of the Kashika branch of the Fuji Bank, Tokyo, Japan, was driving along the Fujishiro by-pass. He had just gone through the towns of Matsudo and Kashiwa, on the Mito road, and was headed for a golf course at Ryugazaki, Ibaraki-ken. (This region lies a little north of Tokyo.) In the car with him were two passengers. These were a Mr. Saito, vice-director of the bank's Kashika branch, and another man who was a client of the bank.

"Ever since passing through a place called Kanamachi, they had in view another car, which was about 150 yards ahead of them and traveling in the same direction. It was a black car, of a type known as the Toyopet New Crown, and it had a Tokyo registration number (which, of course, most unfortunately none of them memorized). In the left-hand rear seat of this black car was an elderly man, who was reading a newspaper. We are given no information about the driver or any other occupants.

"Suddenly, a 'puff of something gaseous, like white smoke or vapor, gushed out from somewhere around the black car' and when this cloud dispersed (a matter of not more than five seconds) the black car had vanished.

"Not having memorized the registration number of the black car, Mr. Kinoshita and his companions felt that there was no way of tracing it, nor of finding out who had been in the car and what had become of them.

"This affair was reported in the evening edition of the *Mainichi* (one of Japan's two leading papers) of March 4, 1964. The newspaper stated that hallucination had been suggestion as an explanation, but all three witnesses vehemently denied that there could have been any question of hallucination."[25]

Many more teleportation cases have come to light in recent years. These have been collected from *Flying Saucer Review*'s many overseas sources and correspondents.

In 1968 a newly married Brazilian couple were on their honeymoon and had stopped for a rest during their journey by car through the southern Brazilian state of Rio Grande do Sul. They were sitting in their Volkswagen when suddenly they were overcome by a powerful drowsiness. (We will see this characteristic again when we refer to the Barney Hill case.) When they recovered consciousness they were in Mexico, like the Vidals before them!

The case of Marcilo Ferraz and his wife is interesting. Señor Marcilo Ferraz, a businessman with a big Brazilian sugar firm, and his wife were driving from São Paulo, in Brazil. Near the border of Brazil and Uruguay they encountered the usual "white cloud" and knew no more till they woke up in Mexico![26]

Two points must strike you about these cases.

(1) The fact that the people teleported invariably end up in Mexico. There may be a good explanation for this strange one-way traffic. We can only speculate. Possibly, this may have something to do with vortices. If you enter into one where a cloud UFO is hovering, you are automatically set

down at a certain spot. I am not an expert on this aspect. Some reader may come up with a good answer. There is so much we do not know and that is one of the reasons why this subject is so absorbing.

(2) All the cases of trips to Mexico involved married couples. Now, here again, we are going to do a little speculation. It has been pointed out that speculation is dangerous and that we should only deal with facts. The point is well taken. However, it is my opinion that speculation is both useful and healthy. It sets the thought processes in operation, and provided that we are not too emphatic in saying "this is the answer," then the use of speculation is justified. We may postulate a theory from our speculation which may later be corroborated by other evidence. It is no use collecting a lot of facts and doing nothing about them.

Now, reverting back to all these teleportation cases involving married couples, let us first consider what happened to the Barney Hills. This was a much publicized affair and occurred earlier in 1961.

This was not a teleportation case but had a great many similarities in other respects. This event has already been covered both in the press and very fully in John G. Fuller's excellent book *The Interrupted Journey,* besides being referred to in an earlier book of my own. However, as it has a special bearing on what we are discussing, let us give a brief outline again here.[27]

Mr. and Mrs. Barney Hill were motoring back from Canada to their home in Portsmouth, New Hampshire. It was on the evening of September 19, 1961, that they saw an unusual "star" in the sky. They argued about it and took turns at looking at the object through binoculars. When it came down to treetop level, Barney got out of the car and entered a field to take a closer look through the binoculars. He observed six beings looking at him through windows of the craft and ran back to the car.

Barney drove off at high speed. Soon afterward a strange bleeping sound came from the back of the car. Then they both began to feel very drowsy. (At this point you will recall the Brazilian honeymoon couple who were suddenly overcome by drowsiness in their Volkswagen.) Later on they heard it again and eventually arrived home at 5:00 A.M.

Later, the Hills began to realize that two whole hours and a distance of about thirty-five miles could not be accounted for on that night. Barney too, had not been well.

Eventually, after consulting various doctors, they were sent to Dr. Benjamin Simons, a qualified neurosurgeon. He treated them with hypnotherapy, putting each of the Hills into a trance separately. Then the whole amazing story emerged.

After the first "bleeping" sounds, their car engine had failed (a common factor when cars come in near contact with UFOs) and the vehicle stopped. The Hills had been led by some beings to the UFO, which was now on the ground.

On board the huge craft the Hills had each been given separately, in different rooms, a medical examination.

They were placed back in their car afterward, a little farther along the route, with their memories of what had transpired blocked out by the "leader" of the alien craft.

It is our speculation that something similar could have happened to the Vidals, the Brazilian honeymoon couple, and to Señor and Señora Marcilo Ferraz. In all these cases their memories were a complete blank as to what had transpired during the teleportation period.

We will, of course, never really know, unless these good people submit to similar hypnotherapy treatment from fully qualified medical men. However, it is certainly intriguing food for thought. Whoever these particular aliens may be who are conducting this kind of research, it is obvious that they are not contenting themselves with just one case, but doing what our own scientists do, corroborating their results with other ones.

8

Levitation and UFOs

The Catholic church has a list of some two hundred saints who were proficient at levitating. That is, flying without wings. Desmond Leslie wrote that St. Teresa of Avila frequently flew in the air and used to take off at the most inconvenient moments.[28]

"On one occasion this happened during the visit of a neighboring abbess, and St. Teresa, from a point near the ceiling, was overheard to chide the Almighty in no uncertain terms for making a spectacle of her."

In more modern times, the American spiritualist Daniel Dunglas Home is credited with having flown out of a window in a London house and back into the room in the presence of reliable witnesses.

He underwent tests of his abilities before Sir William Crookes, and on another occasion for Professor von Boutlerow of the Russian Academy of Science. Both were convinced of Home's genuineness. He died in 1886.[29]

Captain Mackay has pointed out in *Flying Saucer Review* that levitation of humans and objects is a well-known séanceroom phenomenon.

Let us examine possible connections with UFO phenomena. Many of the reported cases involving people being teleported as a result of entering clouds could involve levitation as well. These people may have been drawn up by some form of levitation into UFOs, unless of course, the craft were hovering just above the ground.

Gordon Creighton quotes an interesting case from Venezuela.

"A report dated August 6, 1965, from Caracas, capital of Venezuela, stated that a farmer in that country had seen a 'mysterious object' land on his property and leave behind 'a scorched area forty yards wide in his corn.' 'Three strange beings from outer space' emerged from the machine but, when the farmer began walking toward them, they *were whipped back into it,*' and it took off at once."[30] (Italics mine.)

Possibly, this is a case where levitation was involved. However, in all fairness and objectiveness, we must mention Mr. Creighton's question at the end of the report. He asks if this has any possible connection with another case.

This was near Monte Grande and close to Macias, Province of Entre Rios, Argentina, involving Felipe Martinez, a thirty-seven-year-old shopkeeper. Martinez claimed to have met a little man who got out of an egg-shaped craft wearing a helmet which had two cables linking it to the saucer. Frankly, I should have thought that if someone inside the craft, in an emergency, pulled the cables sharply, the ufonaut would have been decapitated![31]

On Wednesday January 7, 1970, an extraordinary incident took place at 4:45 P.M. in a forest outside the village of Imjarvi, sixteen kilometers from the town of Heinola in southern Finland. A forester, Aarno Heinonen, aged thirty-six, and a farmer, Esko Viljo, aged thirty-eight, were out skiing. Both men were expert skiers and had taken part in athletics. For the record, they are both total abstainers and nonsmokers, and highly regarded in the locality.[32]

They had descended from a small hill and were resting for a while in a glade. Suddenly, they heard a buzzing sound and saw a strange object approaching. *It was surrounded by a luminous red-gray cloud.*

The skiers then saw that the cloudlike object had descended as low as fifty feet, and they could see inside the cloud a round object, flat at the bottom and metalic, with a short tube underneath which extended about eight inches.

Then the object began to buzz even louder and descended still farther. The red-gray mist gradually evaporated. The object was now stationary about ten feet above the ground. The buzzing ceased.

Suddenly, a bright light beam was emitted from the tube under the object. It played around the snow. Then it created a bright illuminated circle about three feet in diameter, while around it was a black edge. A red-gray mist descended over the spot.

Then the two skiers caught sight of the strange little creature who appeared on the ground in the center of the light beam. He had a black box in his hands. He was just under three feet tall, with very thin arms and legs.

While the two men were standing there looking at the creature, it put the opening in the black box toward Heinonen. The light that came from it was almost blinding. A thick red-gray mist came down from the object and red, green, and purple sparks flew out over the area where the two skiers were standing. The mist was now so thick that the two men could not see each other.

Suddenly, the light beam floated upward and went back into the tube of the object, taking the creature with it. The mist dispersed and the object had gone. Unfortunately, both skiers experienced severe internal complaints afterward, which have proved very difficult for the local doctor to diagnose.

The question arises, Was the creature taken back into the UFO by some form of levitation? There are, incidentally, many other cases on record of entities coming down and going back to UFOs on light beams.

Many people and animals have experienced a feeling of weightlessness in the vicinity of UFOs. A South African pilot, Anton Fitzgerald, in an article called *Repeat Performance,* originally published in the South African aviation magazine *Wings over Africa,* subsequently reprinted in *Flying Saucer Review,* gives some examples of this weightlessness.[33]

Mr. Fitzgerald was walking down the hill toward his homestead in Natal accompanied by his farm manager, Jack

Marais. From their position on the hill they could see the landing strip close by the homestead and the large hangar. Mr. Fitzgerald's twin-engined Aero Commander had already been pushed out on to the runway ready for his departure for Durban.

They both saw the eerie reddish glow on the runway at the same time. It was about three hundred yards from the house, and roughly two hundred yards from them.

It was noticeable that the animals around the farm were behaving oddly. "From our elevated position the sheep reminded me of iron filings on a piece of paper around a magnet —a sort of orderly pattern but yet following no accepted geometrical form."

Suddenly, when the two men were "only a stone's throw away" the object rose vertically into the air. There was no sound, no rush of air.

They watched the object disappear into the mist. Jack suddenly exclaimed, "Just look at those sheep!"

Fitzgerald wrote: "I also looked at the sheep and noticed with amazement that they all appeared to be standing on tiptoe like ballet dancers with heads held unusually high just as if they were suspended in space with their hooves barely touching the grass. It was then that we both first experienced a peculiar feeling almost of weightlessness."

After a checkup it was found that one old sheep was missing.

When Fitzgerald took off in the Aero Commander the plane climbed abnormally fast and he found himself "sitting more lightly than usual on his seat."

Almost a year later he had another UFO experience. This time halfway across the world in Texas. On this occasion he was passenger in an MU2 turboprop that the pilot, Jake Rugel, who was part Cherokee Indian, was trying to sell him as a replacement for his old Aero Commander.

They were flying from Love Field, Dallas, to San Angelo, when both of them saw the object at the same time. At first they thought it was a fast-climbing jet, then a large meteorological balloon.

Suddenly, Jake let out a cry that could only have originated way back in some Cherokee wigwam and exclaimed, "Look at that goddarned thing climb!"

Fitzgerald observed that there was the same eerie pinkish glow he had seen a year before on his Natal farm.

Soon after landing, Jake was telephoned by a business contact, a Texas farmer named Ted Leslie, who had been visited by the UFO.

Fitzgerald and Rugel flew over to his farm and were greeted on the runway by Leslie, who related a very similar tale to Fitzgerald's experiences in Natal the year before.

Exactly the same thing had occurred, except that instead of sheep it was whiteface Hereford steers that had stood in a sort of semicircle in the night paddock, only half a mile from his home. There had been the same pinkish glow, the absence of sound, the peculiar weightless feeling, and one of the older steers was missing.

Fitzgerald points out that Ndolwana, his Zulu tractor driver on his farm in Natal, descendant of a Zulu headman, "had now seen for himself, in the flesh so to speak, the foundation of the ancient Zulu legend of the red sun that rises straight up into the sky after devouring some of the tribe's cattle," and across the world in Texas, Jake Rugel, descendant of the Cherokee Indians, and Leslie's cowhand "both were positive that the ancient folklore of the Indian tribes mentions that the 'red sun' invariably appeared among the buffalo herds and the Indians believed that some of the buffalo were carried away."

Our main reason for giving this interesting story from a reliable witness is, of course, its several references to weightlessness and the strange behavior of the animals in both Natal and Texas.

Here indeed, we have reputable evidence supplied by pilots, published in a respectable aviation magazine, which should give us food for thought.

However, some people may ask what all this has to do with levitation. These are examples of the UFOs successfully overcoming gravity. But, what is levitation, if it is not overcoming the limitations of gravity? The saints mentioned earlier, through their excessive ecstasy, somehow or other gyrated to the ceiling. I can't tell you how it was done, and in fact they were not able to control this faculty themselves. St. Teresa was very perturbed about this.

The ufonauts have obviously perfected this ability. They not only understand the laws behind the art of levitation but are in perfect control. That is the difference between them and us.

9

Materialization and UFOs

It is a well-known feature of the séance room for objects to materialize and dematerialize. They are known as apports.

Do UFOs materialize from another order of matter to our own? Do they have the ability to manifest in our physical universe from other, invisible, ones interpenetrating our own?

The late Dr. Meade Layne, with whom I had an extensive correspondence in the nineteen-fifties, published his own findings on this point in a remarkable book, *The Coming of the Guardians.*[34] He called the ufonauts "Etherians" and their particular order of matter "etheric." In 1955, Dr. Layne, in an article specially written for *Flying Saucer Review* called "Mat and Demat," stated:

"Aeroforms are flying discs, saucers, mutants, or indescripts, and best understood with respect to their origin and nature as being *emergents:* that is, they emerge onto our plane of perception from a space-time frame of reference which is different from ours. This process may also be described as a conversion of energy and a change of vibratory rates.

"That this is so is obviously suggested by the phenomena themselves: since physical matter as we know it could not withstand the speed, temperature, and strain imposed by the observed operations of the discs and other forms. This does *not* conflict with the apparent composition of the 'landed' discs.

"When the energy conversion takes place, the aeroform

becomes visible and tangible. It appears to be and definitely *is* what we call solid stance, and so remains until the vibratory rate is again converted. The 'steel' of a landed disc is an etheric steel and its copper is etheric copper—since the prototypes of all our metals exist in etheric matter; nevertheless, chemical analysis has shown certain radical differences. The conversion process amounts to materialization and dematerialization ('Mat and Demat'), 'Demat' on our plane of perception would be 'Mat' for any consciousness functioning on the etheric level, and vice versa.

"Just as there is a spectrum of sound and of color (ending in sounds we cannot hear and colors we cannot see), so there is also a spectrum of tangibility, ending in forms of matter which are too dense to be touched. The ordinary matter of our plane is a rarefaction, and the interspaces between the nucleus and the electrons are relatively enormous. The extremely dense matter of the ethers passes through earth substance freely and almost without friction. But if the vibratory rate of an etheric object is slowed down, it becomes less dense and enters our field of perception."

It is interesting to note that later on Dr. Layne remarks, "Whether the Etherian people are 'human' or not depends on one's definition of the word *human*. So far as we know, they are not excarnate humans and have not lived on our planet, although often visiting it. It is a cardinal mistake to assume that their bodies, and the ether ships created by them, are necessarily the same as we have seen them, when they withdraw to their own plane of existence. It is a cardinal mistake to assume that they are all of the same kind and 'race,' or of the same moral character and evolutionary development."[35]

These last comments bring to mind the words of John A. Keel, the foremost UFO writer and researcher in the United States. In his monumental work, *UFOs—Operation Trojan Horse,* he wrote:

"The Devil and his demons can, according to the literature, manifest themselves in almost any form and can physically imitate anything from angels to horrifying monsters with glowing eyes. Strange objects and entities materialize and dematerialize in the stories, just as the UFOs and their splendid occupants appear and disappear, walk through walls, and perform other supernatural feats."[36]

There have been an overwhelming number of cases where UFOs have suddenly materialized from "nowhere," and numerous instances where alleged ufonauts have appeared to earth people.

In an earlier book I related the story of Mrs. Cynthia Appleton, a Birmingham housewife, who claimed she was visited by Venusians. They materialized and dematerialized in front of her.[37]

An example of an apparent dematerialization of a UFO is described in "The Case of the French Engineers," from Jacques and Janine Vallee's book *Challenge to Science*.[38] The authors stated that the French papers, particularly *France-Soir* and *Le Dauphin Libéré* of September 20, 1957, published accounts of the sighting made by two engineers from Grenoble on September 16, 1957, at about 5:15 P.M. Here is their story.

"We were amazed to see four black craft, which stopped in the sky at a high altitude. They did not have the shape of aircraft or helicopters. They were circular objects that gave the impression that they were swinging in space. I know what balloons are: I experimented with balloons myself. The craft we were observing had nothing in common with these types of balloons.

"Our curiosity reached a peak when one of the objects, all of a sudden, dived vertically at very high speed and then vanished in complete silence. But our emotions were only beginning. There remained three objects clearly visible in the sky. Suddenly, a white object detached itself from one of them and 'floated' for five to seven minutes. Then, abruptly, one of the craft dashed to the west followed by this 'satellite,' which seemed to want to catch up with it. Finally, the last two objects went away vertically and were lost to sight.

"As we were exchanging our observations a fifth object of the same circular shape, and coming from the east, crossed the sky at a high rate of speed and was lost to sight in the sky over St.-Eynard. This was five minutes after the first sighting." (Italics mine.)

What happened to one of the four original objects that suddenly "dived vertically at very high speed and then vanished in complete silence"? Did it enter another order of matter invisible to us mortal beings?

Finally, here is another quote from John Keel which is more food for the little gray cells.

"In psychic phenomena and demonology we find that seemingly solid physical objects are materialized and dematerialized or apported. There are many baffling cases of houses which appeared and disappeared mysteriously. . . .

"Ufologists have constructed elaborate theories about flying saucer propulsion and antigravity. But we cannot exclude the possibility that these wondrous 'machines' are made of the same stuff as our disappearing houses and they don't fly —they levitate. They are merely temporary intrusions into our reality or space-time continuum, momentary manipulations of electromagnetic energy. When they 'lower their frequencies' (as the contactees put it) and enter a solid state, they can leave impressions on the ground. But to enter that state, they need some atoms from our world—parts of an airplane, an auto, or blood and matter from an animal or human being. Or, in some cases, they need to drain off energy from the human percipients or from power lines and automobile engines. This may seem like a fantastic concept, but we have wasted twenty years trying to simplify all this, trying to find a more mundane explanation. . . ."

Mr. Keel's views here are highly controversial but, if accurate, would explain why Mr. Fitzgerald's sheep and Mr. Leslie's steer were taken by UFOs. A horrifying thought. On the other hand, sheep and steers are ultimately slaughtered and eaten by us, anyway.

10

Precipitations and UFOs

Captain Mackay in his *Flying Saucer Review* article referred to "precipitations—angel hair, jelly, oily fluids, etc., which evaporate and disappear. Viscous precipitations and the feeling of hairs being drawn across the face are met with during the production of séance room materialization phenomena."

It is undoubtedly correct that people participating in séances often get a feeling of stickiness and of something oily, although no oil can actually be seen.

There are many instances of oily substances being discovered in areas where a UFO has been seen, close at hand, or even landed.

On November 5, 1955, Reinhold Schmidt, a grain buyer from Bakersfield, California, was driving his car near Kearney, Nebraska. Suddenly, his engine petered out. Nearby, was a strange one-hundred-foot-long object on the ground. He was allowed by the occupants to enter the craft. However, we are not concerned here with giving a long account of this interesting contact story but in reporting that a patch of oily substance was found at the spot. This was not oil as we know it.[39]

Ectoplasm is a very common feature in the séance room. This is the substance of which materializations are formed and which appears prior to a materialization. It can be likened to a liquid plasticine and flows over things in the room, and can elongate itself to great lengths. It is rather like whitish bubble gum.

Now, a substance very common in UFO sightings is known as "angel hair," rather appropriately! It has often been observed to drop from UFOs and drape itself around telegraph wires, hedges and over the countryside.

Aimé Michel, in his first book, *The Truth about Flying Saucers,* described the now classic sightings at Oloron and Gaillac, in France, which took place ten days apart.[40] I think it is essential to include them here because they are perfect examples as far as angel hair goes. To my way of thinking, these two sightings are in a sense really one, as you will see, and there is something quite uncanny about them, which is positively fascinating.

The first sighting took place on Friday, October, 17, 1952, at Oloron. It was an absolutely perfect day with a clear blue sky. The fantastic event was witnessed by Yves Prigent, the head of the Oloron High School, his wife, and their three children.

This is M. Prigent's account of what he and his family saw, taken from Michel's book.

"In the north, a cottony cloud of strange shape was floating against the blue sky. Above it a long narrow cylinder, apparently inclined at a 45° angle, was slowly moving in a straight line toward the southwest. I estimated its altitude as two or three kilometers. The object was whitish, nonluminous, and very distinctly defined. A sort of plume of white smoke was escaping from its upper end. At some distance in front of the cylinder, about thirty other objects were following the same trajectory. To the naked eye, they appeared as featureless balls resembling puffs of smoke. But, with the help of opera glasses it was possible to make out a central red sphere, surrounded by a sort of yellowish ring inclined at an angle. 'The angle,' according to M. Prigent, 'was such as to conceal almost entirely the lower part of the central sphere, while revealing its upper surface. These "saucers" moved in pairs, following a broken path characterized in general by rapid and short zigzags. When two saucers drew away from one another, a whitish streak, like an electric arc, was produced between them.

"*All these strange objects left an abundant trail behind them, which slowly fell to the ground as it dispersed. For several hours, clumps of it hung in the trees, on the telephone wires, and on the roofs of the houses.*'" (Italics mine.)

Michel goes to state that various people were able to collect some of this "gossamer like" substance, which rapidly became gelatinous, sublimed in the air and disappeared.

Ten days later, on October 17, the whole scene was re-enacted again over Gaillac. The same actors, the same play. The long plumed cylinder, inclined at 45° in the midst of a procession of saucers flying in pairs zigzag fashion, and dispersing as at Oleron, large quantities of "angel hair." At Gaillac there were about a hundred witnesses, including two police officers.

We will be referring to these two sightings again later regarding another possible connection with the paranormal.

The late Professor Charles A. Maney, former head of the Department of Physics at Defiance College, Defiance, Ohio, wrote an article some years ago for *Flying Saucer Review,* entitled "The Phenomena of Angel Hair," in which he documented angel-hair cases all over the world, notably in Europe, the United States, Australia, and New Zealand. Since then, there have been numerous other cases.[41]

Now it is possible that angel hair and maybe other oily substances could be superfluous materialized energy left over from the materialization of a UFO from another dimension or space-time continuum.

Further, that this superfluous material, not used, drops to earth and gradually dissolves back into its own dimension. This, of course, I cannot prove; it is only theoretical speculation. However, you might like to ponder on this idea.

If this thought has some interest, it could be compared with ectoplasm to some extent. This, we have seen, is a substance that appears in the séance room and from which materializations manifest. We are not saying that angel hair and ectoplasm are necessarily the same. *However, they may be "cousins."* Angel hair may be a by-product of something more closely connected with ectoplasm. Anyway, these ideas may open up a train of thought for ufologists and another field of research.

11

Expansion and
Contraction of UFOs

"UFOs have appeared as localized points of light and then grown into large quasi-solid objects, only to shrink to pinpoints of light again and disappear. In séance rooms materialization phenomena, ectoplasmic faces, or hands have been observed as being quite tiny and then to have 'grown' to much larger proportions, and later to shrink away (rather like the blowing up of a balloon with a face painted on it and then letting the air out)." (Captain Ivar Mackay, "UFOs and the Occult—1, *Flying Saucer Review*)

Gordon Creighton devotes a chapter in *The Humanoids* to the Villa Santina case, the central figure of which was Professor Rapuzzi Luigi Johannis, a well-known Italian painter and writer.[42]

During the early part of August 1947, Professor Johannis was in a small village called Raveo, near Villa Santina, in Carnia (Friuli) in the extreme northeast of Italy. He regularly visited there each summer searching for fossils, as geology was one of his favorite sciences.

On August 14, he set off early one morning with a small knapsack and his geologist's pick, and was following a path along the left bank of a stream. He passed through some fir trees and then noticed a large, red lenticular object. The professor is shortsighted, so he put on his glasses and noticed it was a disc about thirty feet wide, and about twenty feet above the stream.

He then saw what at first seemed to be two boys. He shouted to them, pointing to the disc and walked toward them. Then he stopped, petrified.

The two boys were "dwarfs," "the likes of which I had never seen or imagined," stated the professor. They were no more than three feet in height and wearing what appeared to be dark-blue overalls made of some material the professor could not describe. " 'Translucent' is the only word for it," he said.

He gazed at them in astonishment for what seemed a long time. Then, unfortunately, he raised his arm with the pick and waved it in their direction, shouting out to ask if he could be of any help to them.

The beings must have thought he was threatening them, for one raised his right hand to his belt and from it came something like a ray which felled the professor to the ground. His pick shot out of his hand "as though snatched by an invisible force."

The two beings came over quite close to him and one of them picked up the tool. Then they made their way back to the disc. After a few minutes the object rose into the air.

After a time, it tipped slightly away from its vertical position. *Then it suddenly grew smaller, and vanished.*

Eventually, the professor recovered sufficiently to make his way home.

In a footnote Gordon Creighton wrote: "The disc 'grew smaller before it vanished.' One feels there is something of fantastic importance here, a tremendous clue. Captain Howard told me that his gigantic UFO seen over the Atlantic in 1954, seemed to grow smaller while remaining at the same distance from the observers. In the Whidby Island case of October 1963, the gray ten-foot-long craft, shaped more like a wing airplane than a disc, 'suddenly shrank considerably in size and tilted so that its rear portion dipped into the ground.' Professor Johannis's disc was also tipped up in a strange way and sticking into the rock. For heaven's sake, will all our experts on tempic fields and the plurality of dimensions please put their thinking caps on about these cases!"

Frankly, I think the granddaddy of all these expansion and contraction cases is the extremely well authenticated one involving aircraft of the Portuguese Air Force. A long account has been given elsewhere, so we will content ourselves with an abridged version to bring out the salient points under consideration.[43]

A flight of four jet fighter-bombers took off from Ota Air Base, Portugal, on a routine practice night flight, on September 4, 1957. They were under the command of Captain José Lemos Ferreira.

The first part of the flight went as scheduled. Then Captain Ferreira noticed an unusual light above the horizon and alerted the other pilots. After the UFO underwent various color changes, suddenly, according to Captain Ferreira, *the object enlarged, becoming five or six times its initial size.* Before the pilots had time to get over that spectacle, *the object shrank becoming a barely visible, small yellowish point.*

After about seven or eight minutes of these changes in size, the UFO had been gradually getting down below the horizon. Soon afterward, Captain Ferreira decided to abandon the mission and head back to base, as nobody was now paying any attention to the exercise.

The UFO had now turned bright red. Suddenly they spotted four other objects which had apparently come out of the mother ship.

Then wow! The leading UFO dived and soared up rapidly in their direction. Then, Captain Ferreira reported, everyone went wild and almost broke formation in the process of getting across and ahead of the climbing UFO. As soon as they had crossed over the path of the UFO, the objects began to disappear, and the squadron landed without further incident. The total sighting lasted forty minutes.

At the time, I was editor of *Flying Saucer Review.* Our Lisbon correspondent was successful in obtaining an interview with Captain Ferreira, at Ota Air Base. The captain's personal account, together with photographs of the three sergeant pilots and himself, was published in the *Review*. Quite a scoop, really, as this exciting story involved military personel.

It is amazing that this excellent high-caliber sighting is not given a mention in the Condon Report. However, from the standpoint of expansion and contraction of objects you could not have a more perfect example.

12

Animals and UFOs

In this chapter we will consider the effect of UFOs on animals. This was not one of the items listed by Captain Mackay in his *FSR* article, but we feel it should be included in this section of the book on the paranormal aspect of the UFOs.

We have already touched upon animal behavior in the vicinity of UFOs, in describing the odd reactions of Mr. Fitzgerald's sheep and Mr. Leslie's steers.

The most comprehensive collection of cases in this category has recently appeared in a series of articles called "A New FSR Catalogue" by Gordon Creighton in *Flying Saucer Review*. The amount of reading and research needed to collect over two hundred cases of this nature must have been tremendous. Mr. Creighton has rendered ufology a signal service with this fine piece of work.[44]

The catalogue starts with an incident from the reign of Alexander the Great, in which two strange craft dived repeatedly at his army, causing the elephants and horses to panic. Although many of the cases in the catalogue may well have a bearing on the paranormal aspect, some may not. Indeed, the writer of the catalogue is obviously well aware of this point. In his introduction he states that many of the incidents quoted, involving panic on the part of animals, may be due to some other cause.

The panicking of the elephants and horses belonging to Alexander's army was not necessarily caused because the two

/ 77

diving craft emanated from an alien dimension. If two modern, military jet fighter aircraft were to repeatedly dive over an army containing elephants and horses today, no doubt a similar stampede among the animals would result.

However, when we take all the two hundred or so cases listed in the catalogue, there is a distinct a priori case for paranormal influences being involved.

When modern aircraft pass over fields where cattle and sheep are grazing there is no particular disturbance. The animals go on nibbling the pasture or continue whatever they were doing, completely unruffled.

On the other hand, when UFOs appear in their vicinity, the animals exhibit extreme alarm and fright. It could be argued that the animals are now used to modern aircraft. The point is well taken. However, there are many different types of aircraft in the skies—small private airplanes; great airliners; military jet fighters; helicopters; and, finally, balloons and gliders. The variety is enormous. Occasionally, new types of aircraft are seen. None of these seem to unduly worry the animals.

If the UFOs were simply plainly extraterrestrial, that is, from other planets in our physical universe, then their craft would surely not cause such concern to the animals, who, after all, are used to seeing a large variety of aircraft in the skies.

The implications to be gotten from the collected cases in Creighton's catalogue are that the animals become genuinely alarmed when UFOs appear for one good solid reason. They instinctively *know* that the UFOs are alien in the sense that the substance of the ships and the occupants comes from another dimension than our own. Not only "out of this world" but out of our space-time continuum!

It is well known that animals are far more psychic than the average human being. Cats and dogs are famed for this sixth sense.

Creighton quotes the case of a dog from Aimé Michel's book. This is Case No. 34, Quarouble, France, 10:30 P.M., September 10, 1954.

"Attention of Marius Dewilde was attracted by the howling of his dog outside. 'Howling enough to awaken the dead.' When he opened the door, the dog came crawling toward him in abject terror. (UFOs and creatures were then encountered by him outside the house)."

Another case involving dogs is No. 38 in the catalogue, Poncey-sur-l'Ignon, France, 8 P.M., October 2, 1954.

"Mme. Guainet was milking her cows in the byre, when her dogs, which usually stayed near her while she milked, rushed out toward the woods, baying. She followed, and saw a vast illuminated 'cigar' craft, flying low." (The source of this case is also M. Michel's book.)

The same year, 1954, which was a UFO 'flap' one in France, included this case involving cows.

Case No. 40, Bauquay, Calvados, France, dawn, October 11, 1954.

"A Normandy farmer was on his way across the fields to milk his cow. With two other witnesses, he watched a huge red elongated object, brightly illuminated, sweep toward them at treetop height. The terrified cows in the various fields scattered in all directions, their bells jangling wildly. When the UFO had vanished and the farmer had caught his cow, neither he nor the other farmers could coax a drop of milk out of her, and she gave none until the morning of the following day." (The source of this case is also M. Michel's book, p. 159.)

The next case, No. 65 in the catalogue, is well recalled, as at the time I was editor of *Flying Saucer Review,* and corresponded with Commander J. O. S. Wilde, R.N. (Ret.) in Ghana about the occurrence. Here it is:

Keta, near Accra, Ghana, nights of April 8–9 and 9–10, 1958.

"Commander J. O. S. Wilde, R.N. (Ret.), at that time acting as area investigator in Ghana for *Flying Saucer Review,* was awakened at 3:30 A.M. on April 9 by the loud barking of dogs, quacking of ducks, and general pandemonium among all animals and birds. He then noticed a bright light which rose up into the sky from the sea with a sort of 'bobbing motion.'

He watched the light for one hour and was able to establish that it was the cause of the great excitement among animals and birds. The same thing occurred again at 3:30 A.M. on April 10, the alarm again being given by the dogs and ducks." (The source is *Flying Saucer Review,* September-October 1958, p. 6.)

The uncanny influence that UFOs seem to have over both the animal and bird kingdoms whenever they make an appearance is well exemplified in the following incident.

Case No. 67, Rio Pardo, Mato Grosso, Brazil, June 1959.

"Three men were hunting crocodiles at night in a boat on this river. Suddenly, a large circular UFO appeared, halted over the opposite bank, protruded a long tube in their direction from the center of its under portion, and they felt that they were being scrutinized. *The feature which unnerved most of all, however, was the 'awful, uncanny silence' which suddenly descended on the tropical forest, usually so loud with varied forms of life even at night.* Not a cicada was to be heard while the experience lasted, all sound seeming to be blotted out as if by a curtain." (Italics mine. From the *Flying Saucer Review,* July-August 1967, p. 6.)

In an earlier chapter we covered the Barney Hill abduction by UFO entities. Another aspect of this case, involving their dog, is included in Creighton's catalogue.

Case No. 72, New Hampshire, night of September 19, 1961.

"Their dachshund Delsey was in the car. The various references to the dog in the course of the hypnosis sessions indicate that the animal had become very disturbed as soon as the UFO appeared in the sky. They at first had interpreted this as simply meaning that the dog needed to be put out for a run, but the hypnosis now showed that this was not so and that the dog's condition had grown considerably worse. By the time that they were flagged down by the party of beings from the landed UFO, the dog was lying in a tight tense ball under the seat, trembling violently. When they returned after their experiences with the entities, they found the dog still cowering there in the same condition." (Source: John G. Fuller's *The Interrupted Journey*, pp. 6, 12, 93, 123, 136, 178.)

Here is an interesting Australian case, Case No. 75, Moe, Australia (7 A.M., February 15, 1963.)

"Farmer Charles Brew and his son Trevor were in the dairy when a thick gray disc about twenty-five feet wide, with protrusions and a dome on top, came shooting straight down toward the farm and to a height of only seventy-five or a hundred feet, during rain. It threw all the animals into a panic. Horses reared up and cows turned somersaults. Many of the cattle broke out and had to be rounded up. All were affected for some days, and would not reenter the paddock over which the UFO had hovered briefly. The sound made by the UFO was 'a whistling, like the whistling of a turbine.'" (*Flying Saucer Review*. May–June 1963, p. 63.) This was one of the cases presented by Dr. James McDonald on March 12, 1968, before the Symposium of the Canadian Aeronautical and Space Institute in Montreal.

Our next case shows a distinct connection with psychic phenomena and is worthy of inclusion here. Case No. 76, Boskloof, Cape Province, South Africa, April–May 1963.

"An outbreak of UFO and poltergeist phenomena kept the small farming community of Boskloof, near Clanwilliam, in an uproar. There were many reports of herds of cattle being frightened by red glowing lights, of dogs fleeing in terror from strange noises, appearances of ghostly figures, falling stones (a typical poltergeist phenomenon), etc." ("Flying Saucer Scare in the Cape," *Flying Saucer Review*, July–August 1963.)

The following report is loaded with poltergeist overtones and comes from the quiet, sleepy town of Warminster, Wiltshire, England, the scene of much UFO activity.

Case No. 85, Warminster, England, 6:12 A.M., December 25, 1964, and on subsequent dates.

"Among the numerous 'UFO phenomena' or 'poltergeist-type phenomena' reported from Warminster and vicinity it may be noted that, at or near the outset, at just after 6 A.M. on Christmas day, a young married couple claim that they were awakened by the frantic barking and whimpering of their dog in the garden outside. Josie, their daughter, went to investigate, and found the dog lying in a corner of the woodshed, trembling and whimpering. Just as Josie was about to reenter the house she experienced, as it were from the air right overhead, the terrifying, 'whining, crackling, rasping, droning, shattering phenomenon' which later became known throughout the world as 'the Warminster Thing.' At around the same period there also occurred a case in which a flock of pigeons allegedly fell dead near Warminster, struck down by this mysterious force, *rigor mortis* supervening in the bodies almost at once. The same informant claimed that on yet another occasion large numbers of dead fieldmice had been found on the ground just after the passage overhead of 'The Thing,' their bodies riddled with tiny holes." ("The Warminster Phenomenon," *Flying Saucer Review,* July–August 1965. See also various Warminster press reports, 1964–65.)

There is a saying "that enough is as good as a feast," and we will content ourselves with just two more cases from Gordon Creighton's collection.

Case No. 99, Kensington, New Hampshire, night of September 3, 1965.

"The famous Muscarello case. Dogs howled frantically and horses inside a barn whinnied and kicked madly at their stalls as a large red UFO was flying overhead, very low." (The horses, being *inside* the building, will certainly not have been able to *see* the UFO.) (John G. Fuller, *Incident at Exeter,* Chapter 1.)

Case No. 122, Haynesville, Louisiana, 8:15 P.M., December 30, 1966:

"An American nuclear physicist was driving south with his family. The weather was overcast and it was raining. At a point just before they reached Haynesville they saw, stationary in the forest, either just before the treetops or at ground level, a pulsating dome of light which alternated between a dim red and a bright orange. At one moment its luminosity suddenly became far brighter than the car's headlights, and awoke the scientist's two children, who had been asleep on the back seats. The scientist (a professor of physics as well as a nuclear researcher) made some rapid calculations of the amount of energy represented by the light, and was so impressed that he returned to the area the next day with a scintillometer, and was able to determine the position of the light as having been about one mile from his car at the nearest point.

"Then, while walking in the forest, he noted that for a considerable distance around the landing site, all animal life appeared to have utterly vanished. There were no squirrels, no birds, not even any insects, and as a keen hunter he was himself familiar with the abundant Louisiana fauna. Finally, on inquiring among local people who had also seen the light, he made the startling discovery that important losses of cattle had occurred that same night. He also detected traces of burns on the ground. He reported the matter to both the U.S. Air Force and the Condon Commission at the University of Colorado." (Jacques Vallée, *Passport to Magonia,* pp. 45, 338.)

In concluding this chapter I would like to make the following observations. Domestic animals (not cats and dogs) should really be afraid of us because, as I have pointed out earlier, they usually end up as steaks and shoulders of lamb for our tables. Probably, when grazing placidly in the fields, they have no inkling of their ultimate fate.

This, then, makes it all the more interesting that they should show such fright when a UFO is in the vicinity. They seem to know instinctively that UFOs are something different —something not basically physical as we know it—from the variety of aircraft usually to be seen in our skies.

There is another aspect that should be taken into account when studying the effects of UFOs on animals. The spectrum of human hearing extends from twenty cycles to fifteen thousand cycles per second. It is a well-known fact that animals can hear sounds beyond both ends of the spectrum of human hearing.

It could be that when a UFO is hovering or moving slowly overhead the animals can hear the sound to such an unbearable degree that it causes them to go all taut, as in the case of Barney Hill's dog Delsey. You will recall that the poor creature rolled up into a terrified, tense ball.

Then, when the UFO moves off suddenly at ultrasonic speed, that is with a sound so high-pitched as to be beyond the range of human hearing, but still within that of the animals, the effect on the latter could be devastating.

Therefore, I suggest that a good deal of the fright experienced by the animal world could be due to the terrible sounds at both ends of the sound spectrum. It seems to me that both subsonics and ultrasonics play a large part in the effect of UFOs on animals.

This does not invalidate the concept that some of the UFOs came from invisible universes. The two ideas are possibly interrelated.

13

Telepathy and Cloud UFOs

Telepathy was not one of the subjects included by Captain Mackay in his *FSR* article. I have since learned that in his view this was more a mental faculty than a paranormal one. On the other hand, one of the early pioneer workers in the telepathic field, Dr. J. B. Rhine, has long held the view that telepathy is nonphysical. In some ways, too, it has close links with telekinesis, a subject listed by Captain Mackay. So, we feel it is important to discuss telepathy here.

According to Webster's Third New International Dictionary, the etymology of the word *telepathy* is as follows: *Tele,* a combining form from Greek, meaning far, far off, distant; and -*pathy,* a combining form from Greek meaning to experience, suffer.

It is now some years since the pioneering work of Dr. J. B. Rhine at Duke University, in the United States, and that of Dr. J. S. Soal at Cambridge University, in England. Since then, a great deal of progress has been made. Both the United States and Russian military authorities are known to be working overtime on paranormal research, including telepathy.

Louis Pauwels and Jacques Bergier, in their remarkable book *Morning of the Magicians,* disclosed that early in 1957 the famous Rand organization, which was engaged on some most secret research work for the United States government, submitted a report on this subject to President Eisenhower. It contained the following statement: "Our submarines are useless to us now, because it is impossible to communicate with them when they are submerged, especially when in polar waters. All-new means of communication must be employed."[45]

The authors of *Morning of the Magicians* went on to state that no action was taken for a year because the recommendations seemed too much like table-turning. However, when the Russians put up Sputnik 1 into space the U.S. authorities changed their minds.

Two men took part in a fantastic experiment. One embarked on the submarine *Nautilus* on July 25, 1959. The submarine at once put to sea and remained submerged for sixteen days on its journey across the Atlantic.

The other man, a student at Duke University, remained shut up in a room for the whole period, sitting in front of an automatic machine in which a thousand cards were being continually shaken up. These were Zener cards, used for paranormal experiments.

When a card was ejected by the machine the student would stare fixedly at it and concentrate upon the markings.

Fifteen hundred miles away far below the surface of the ocean our man in the submarine tried to guess the card. He wrote down the result, which was countersigned by the commanding officer.

The final result. *Seven times out of ten,* the man in the submarine had "guessed" correctly!

The U.S.S.R. has an official laboratory in Leningrad conducting research into extra sensory perception, including telepathy.

We have gone to some pains to indicate that telepathy is now taken very seriously by scientists and the military authorities, both in the West and in the East. Now, if we can take telepathy as a scientific fact, then some of the contactee reports that have been reported over the last two decades in which telepathic communication is involved, should also be regarded a little more seriously than hitherto.

It is important to realize a point that stands out in regard to telepathic communication between ufonauts and our own people. There tends to be among those potentially telepathic on this planet a slant toward being receivers rather than senders. For instance, in the annals of ufology there is case after case where some person "felt an impulse" to go up a hill or to some particular spot.

There is the classic story of Stephen Darbishire. He suddenly felt an urge to go up into the fells on the lower slopes of Coniston Old Man in the Lake District on a damp day in February, 1954. He took his eight-year-old younger brother, Adrian, with him. The idea was to go birdwatching. Stephen took his box camera along too. They might be able to get some snaps of birds.[46]

As they climbed the slopes, Adrian suddenly caught Stephen by the arm and pointed to a saucer-shaped object flying straight down toward them. Stephen managed to get two photographs of the object. One of these, showing the UFO hovering just above the ground, still remains one of the best pictures ever taken of a flying saucer.

Here is a report from Huanuco, Peru:

"At 5 A.M. on September 1, 1965, a foreigner who was unwilling to give his name for publication saw a UFO of oval shape land, at very close range, on an airstrip belonging to a big estate. An entity emerged, some three feet centimeters high, and with a head twice the size of ours. Seeing the man, the creature began to gesticulate and make signs as though trying to communicate. Failing to make himself understood, the being reentered the machine, which became luminous and then vanished straight up into the sky.

"The interesting point is that, beforehand, the man had experienced a strange sensation which seemed to impel him to go to the spot where the craft had landed."[47] (Mr. Donald Hanlon, who forwarded this account to *Flying Saucer Review,* states that his Peruvian correspondent knows the witness in the above story.)

There are numerous other examples of people who have

felt impelled to go to a certain spot, where they came upon a landed UFO. Additionally, there are many cases on record of contactees having telepathic conversations with UFO entities —Adamski, Bethurum, Derenberger, and many others. Their accounts can be read in other books.

When I earlier described a personal sighting of a UFO, reference was made to the fact that after the object had gone my head was full of ideas. It could be argued that this was a coincidence or that the high state of excitement produced by witnessing a UFO caused me to think very rapidly about the subject. All I know is that my head was full of ideas.

There have been other people who have received inspiration and ideas through either seeing a UFO or having a contact. A person who comes to mind is the late Wilbert B. Smith, former head of the Canadian Project Magnet.

If the ufonauts can impress upon someone an impulse to go up a hill or to go out of doors and look up into the sky, then it is more than probable that they can go further and inject the germ of an idea which will trigger off a whole train of thought.

Most people are potentially telepathic. It seems that our telepathic faculty is lying latent in us, but like muscles that have not been used for some time, it has atrophied.

We rely now so much on material communication systems —on the telephone, the cable, and the telegraph, and above all, on language—that our telepathic ability has been neglected. All these communication systems are really extensions outwardly of what we already possess inside us!

It would appear that the ufonauts, many of them, are skilled in the art of telepathy. This is their basic method of communication among themselves. Some even speak our languages. That should not present any great difficulty as they have probably monitored our radio and TV program for some decades. What they must make of them, heaven only knows!

14

The "Windows" and UFOs

The controversy continues over whether the UFOs are extra-terrestrial in origin—that is, from other planets in the galaxy —or whether they come from invisible universes interpenetrating our own. The answer may be a mixture of both these theories.

During the last twenty-five years UFOs have been seen over atomic research stations, military installations, airports, the oceans, lakes, and rivers, cities, hospitals, schools, farms, and isolated areas. You name it. The UFOs have observed everything. They have buzzed our aircraft and paced automobiles and have even been seen to dive into the sea. Earlier, we stated that our astronauts have seen them many times and photographed them.

However, one point has steadily emerged over the years: they seem to have concentrated persistently over centers of magnetic deviation—that is, where there are magnetic faults on the earth's surface. At first it was thought that they were watching those areas that are prone to earthquakes. There was some justification for this thinking, as many UFOs have been spotted flying around such areas after an earthquake. For instance, UFOs were seen over the Midlands in Britain on February 11 and 12, 1957. Five tadpole-shaped objects were observed in the Mansfield area after earth tremors there.[48]

The new thinking on this is that these areas of magnetic deviation are in many cases actually "windows" through which the UFOs manifest to our vision.

Now, it is appreciated that this idea may be difficult for the average person to accept. Fair enough. However, the very idea of spacecraft, not made on earth, coming from somewhere else, is difficult to accept too, for many people. This subject is vast, quite outside the ken of most people, and that is what makes it so fascinating. When the truth is finally known it will turn out to be even more fantastic than any science-fiction tale. Let us not forget that many of the ideas expressed by old-time science-fiction writers such as H. G. Wells and Jules Verne have now come about in real life. Someone once stated that nothing is impossible. The impossible only takes a little longer to come about!

Now, the UFOs have persistently been seen over many "window" areas on the earth. The famous "Bermuda Triangle" in the Gulf of Mexico is a good example.[49] In a recent book of mine it was related how many U.S. Air Force planes, and a subsequent rescue plane sent to find them, all disappeared without a trace. Further instances of both planes and ships disappearing in this area are on record.[50]

Another well-known "window" is the "Devil's Triangle" in the Pacific, near Japan. John A. Keel has listed in the U.S.A. the following ones: Kearney, Nebraska; Wanaque, New Jersey; and Ravenna, Ohio, although he adds that there are actually one or two "windows" in each state.[51]

There is a well-known *fault* line which runs down the whole of the West Coast of North America and extends into South America. This is the San Andreas fault line going through California. (San Francisco had a terrible earthquake in 1906.) It continues down through the Andes into Peru. (In 1970 a catastrophic earthquake occurred in Peru resulting in seventy thousand dead or missing and at least one million homeless.)

Draw a line on a map from Lake Titicaca, which is situated on the borders of Peru and Bolivia, to Caracas, the capital city of Venezuela. Incidentally, Lake Titicaca is a highly significant area. Nearby is the Gate of the Sun at Tiahuanaca, twelve thousand feet up in the High Andes. No one knows for certain how this extraordinary edifice came to be built with two-hundred-ton stones and bearing on its facade a most remarkable calendar which M. Kazantzev, the Russian scientist, stated was not of this earth, but Venusian!

Then, draw another line from Cuzco, also in Peru, to Caracas, in Venezuela. The segment that you have just outlined is a remarkable area where numerous landings have occurred, and is full of countless terraces and enchanting valleys. Most of the area is little explored.

In England, there is Warminster, Wiltshire, already referred to in another chapter, where many UFO sightings, landings, and poltergeist activities have been reported during the last few years. It is significant that on Lord Bath's estate at Longleat, Warminster, there is an area known as "Heaven's Gate"!

There are many more "windows." The Himalayas, the Gobi Desert, the Dordogne area in France, and many others.

It is now thought that due to a warp in the magnetic field around these "window" areas the UFOs are able to manifest from other space-time continuums.

The most informed study in depth of these "windows" has been made by Ivan T. Sanderson, the famed scientist and naturalist. An account of his work with other scientists in this field is given in his remarkable book *Invisible Residents.* [52]

The "windows" mentioned so far in this chapter, with two exceptions, are minor ones, compared with what Sanderson terms "vile vortices."

He pointed out that both the "Bermuda Triangle" and the "Devil's Triangle" are misnamed, because neither of these areas is triangular, but lozenge-shaped, and the so-called Bermuda Triangle is not centered on the island of Bermuda at all.

Sanderson and his friends have discovered a total of ten major lozenge-shaped "vile vortices" spread over the world with what appears to be an extraordinary mathematical precision: three of them in a line between 30° and 40° north latitude, and three in a line between 30° and 40° south latitude. However, there are ten altogether, placed around the globe in such a way that each is opposite another on the other side of the world.

I do not wish to elaborate more on Sanderson's fantastic discoveries, as you should read his fascinating book for yourself.

Suffice it to say that in nearly all these areas planes have mysteriously disappeared, and ships have vanished or been found drifting without a trace of their crews.

Whether the "vile vortices" are places where UFOs manifest from another, invisible, universe remains to be proven. All we can do is point out that these anomalies exist on the earth's surface. Perhaps one day we will know the answer.

Nevertheless, although it is possible that some UFOs do come from other planets in our galaxy—perhaps, as we shall discuss in a later chapter, by traveling through what science-fiction writers call hyperspace—it is now thought that many of the UFOs do come from invisible universes. That is what this book is all about. You are being asked to stretch your thinking processes as never before, but I hope you will enjoy the exercise and stay the course.

15

Further Thoughts
on the Paranormal

Considerable space in this book has been devoted to similarities in both UFO and psychic phenomena. We have taken several of the items listed by Captain Ivar Mackay in his *Flying Saucer Review* article, namely, teleportation; levitation; materializations and dematerializations; precipitations; and finally, expansion and contraction of UFOs. Additionally, we have included three more chapters not listed by Captain Mackay: the effects on animals; telepathy; and "windows."

This finishes our study to show up a possible link between UFOs and the psychic world. In this section of the book I have not set out to definitely prove that there is a connection. In fact, like Captain Mackay in his article, we are only pointing up the similarities and have highlighted some examples of UFO activity which it was not possible for the author of the article in the *Review* to do with the space at his disposal. However we do feel that more than an a priori case for a connection between the two fields has been established.

I have one thought to pass on to you for what it is worth. It seems that the same energy, radiation—call it what you wish—is the force used in all these phenomena, teleportation, levitation, materializations, and so forth. I suggest that basically the same subtle force is being used, perhaps in a different way in all these aspects of the paranormal; the various phenomena seem to be interrelated. For instance, let us take telekinesis. Telekinesis means, roughly, the influence of an animate being on an inanimate object—in short, the ability, for example, to concentrate on a stone and cause it to move without touching it. This surely has a close connection with the ability of a ufonaut to place in a human being's mind an urge to go up a hill or to some other place that the latter had no intention of going before receiving the impulse.

Another interesting possibility that I have not broached before, is that the ufonauts are able in some way to project mental pictures. A possible example of this might be found in the two extraordinary French sightings at Oleron and Gaillac described earlier. It has always struck me as quite uncanny how the same scene, the same actors, the same actions, without an iota of difference, was gone through at Gaillac, ten days after the first sighting. *There is something crying out to be learned here, I feel sure.*

Now, it is up to researchers in both fields to take the matter further. An interesting thought is that it may ultimately turn out that *all* psychic phenomena actually emanates from the UFOs, and not the other way round, as is commonly supposed. After all, if the UFO occupants live in other space-time continuums and can manipulate psychic phenomena, then perhaps they exercise more power over our destinies than we realize. John Keel, the American ufologist, in his book *UFOs: Operation Trojan Horse,* wrote that we are being manipulated by both the "goodies" and "baddies" alike, and that some sort of cosmic mental battle is going on for the control of the minds of mankind.

There may be some truth in all this, but man does have some free will, limited though it may be, and if he keeps his thoughts and consciousness tuned in to the highest state of awareness that is in his capacity, then it is possible to be master of his own destiny.

PART THREE

Wheels
Within Wheels

16

The Mystery Airships

Three major cigar "flaps" occurred just before the turn of the century and within the first decade of this one.

During 1896–97 numerous airships were seen in the skies over large areas of the United States. In my book *Operation Earth,* this "flap" was briefly mentioned:

"If we bear in mind that Count Ferdinand von Zeppelin's first airship was tested in June 1900, when it attained a speed of eighteen m.p.h., and traveled a distance of three and a half miles before an accident to the steering gear caused the flight to be discontinued, then a great black airship that appeared over Kansas City, Missouri, in April 1897 was a little before its time!

"It was seen by ten thousand people. The craft appeared very swiftly, then appeared to stop and hover over the city for ten minutes and after flashing green-blue and white lights, shot upward into space.

"This 'airship' was obviously capable of a very high performance far beyond the primitive zeppelin to be tested three years later. Indeed, even in World War I, the German Zeppelins often had the greatest difficulty in finding their way back to Germany after raids over England."

During that amazing year, 1897, there were many obvious hoaxes, just as there are now nearly three quarters of a century later. Donald B. Hanlon, in an article "The Airship . . . Fact and Fiction," published in *Flying Saucer Review,* analyzed some reports of that extraordinary year. However, after taking into account obvious fakes and misidentifications due to astronomical causes, and mythical accounts written by unscrupulous journalists of the period, Mr. Hanlon concluded, "After sifting through data . . ., one is left with a hard core of sightings (now over two hundred) of a rather unlikely-looking aerial craft which created much commotion among the observers. The only detectable effect the sightings left on the society of 1896–97 is exactly the same as that left by the modern UFO phenomena—a psychological impact.

"It is clear that the origin of the airship is still very much an open issue. It is also clear that the mystery surrounding its appearance at that particular time in history has deepened."[53]

Mr. Hanlon's last paragraph is extremely interesting. Why indeed did the big black cigars appear over the United States at that moment in time, just prior to the birth of the zeppelin? Capable, too, of a fantastic performance.

Another thing to be noticed about that amazing period was the absence of modern UFO shapes and sizes. There were no circular, triangular, crescent-, and cone-shaped UFOs in evidence during that time. They were to come much later.

Let us now turn our attention to two more major cigar "flaps" which occurred in 1909. During March, April and May of that year, these mysterious airships were seen over Britain. However, in the second part of the year they made dramatic appearances over New Zealand!

Carl Grove has described the 1909 wave over Britain in *Flying Saucer Review*.[54] He wrote:

"The 1909 airship was a dark, cigar-shaped object carrying a rather bright 'searchlight' about a hundred feet in length, which maneuvered with ease. Like its 1897 predecessor, it is the behaviour and not the appearance of the airship that connects it with the modern UFO phenomenon. . . ."

Let us quote three of the reports from Mr. Grove's collection.

"May 9. Southend-on-Sea, Essex. Miss H. M. Boville.

" 'I was closing the window of my bedroom, which faces northeast, at about 11:20, when I noticed a very dark object looming out of the sky, and traveling slowly from the direction of Shoeburyness. At first I thought it was the gunpowder cloud that one sees after an explosion, it was so opaque and black, and the night was too dark to enable me to see it clearly. After a few seconds, however, it crossed the sky and remained nearly stationary in front of my window. I could see the outline of a torpedo-shaped airship, very long and large. It was not more than a quarter of a mile above the houses and trees, and remained immovable for a few minutes, then rose higher, and traveled very swiftly in a westerly direction toward the coast and London, showing, as it did so, two very powerful searchlights at either end for a second or two. I did not hear any sound from the engines, as it was too far off, nor could I discern the aeronauts; but the vessel seemed to travel very steadily and smoothly.' " (*Evening News,* May 15, 1909.)

"May 14, North Sea. The steamer *St. Olaf.*

"A Norwegian trading vessel was a short way out from Blyth, Northumberland, when a large airship carrying five searchlights suddenly appeared. Hovering above the *St. Olaf,* it directed all its lights on to the steamer's bridge. It was within hail, Captain Egenes reported, but gave no answer to the challenge, and in the glare of the searchlights no detail could be seen.

"Suddenly, the airship swung off after another steamer a mile or so away, and directed the searchlights upon that. It afterward made off at a sharp rate towards the south." (*East Anglian Daily Times,* May 19, 1909)

"May 15. Newport, Monmouth.

"G. Beanland and A. V. Day, at the local flour mill, sighted a cigar-shaped object *stationary* over Newport Bridge, shortly after 1:00 A.M. Searchlights flashed from each end on to the bridge. After ten minutes one of the lights went out, and the object flew off toward Stow Hill." (South Wales Daily News, Cardiff, May 17, 1909. Italics mine.)

Altogether, Mr. Grove included some forty-three reports in his survey of the 1909 cigar flap over Britain. Once again, there are questions to be asked. Our own airships capable of any reasonable performance did not appear until some years later. Therefore, what were black cigar-shaped airships with powerful searchlights, capable of hovering for long periods and moving off at high speed, doing over Britain in 1909?

The action now shifts to New Zealand. We cannot do better than give you extracts from the account of Mr. Henk J. Hinfelaar, director of New Zealand Scientific Space Research and editor of *Spaceview*.[55]

"Through the excellent cooperation of a reporter on our main daily newspaper, we have been able to unearth a series of sighting reports that would make any skeptic think twice in regard to the existence of unidentified flying objects.

"The period in which these sightings were recorded was devoid of any air traffic other than the earliest efforts of the Wright brothers and Count Zeppelin. The former made their first flight in 1903, while the latter launched his first dirigible in 1900. The second ship of this type was destroyed in 1905, during an emergency landing. Although airship traffic dates from 1909, and was later used for bombing purposes in World War I, none of these dirigibles are known to have visited New Zealand.

"At any rate, the flying range of these craft was so restricted that they had difficulty in making the return flight from Germany to England. Moreover, these ships were cumbersome and their maneuverability was low.

"Having regard to these facts, it was therefore startling, to say the least, when in the year 1909 cigar-shaped flying objects were reported all over New Zealand. The first of these sightings was observed in the last week of July, and the last sighting was reported in the first week of September. For a solid six weeks hundreds of eyewitnesses continued to report the presence of 'phantom' airships in our skies. Sightings were not merely restricted to the craft themselves, but also included (in many cases) their occupants. Dozens of accounts were reported to the local newspapers and in all but a couple of cases the actual sightings could be corroborated by several witnesses.

"As far as localities go, the objects were seen in the North as well as in the South Island, covering an area from Dargaville to Invercargill, a distance of approximately 850 miles. Sightings occurred during the day—as well as at night, and the most outstanding feature in nearly all reports was the description of the unidentified flying object. Never at any stage was more than one object sighted at the same time. The shape of the object was usually described as being elongated ('torpedo,' 'boat,' 'cigar,' or 'codfish').

"In some cases, always at night, the objects carried strong searchlights (with reflectors) which lit up the landscape for miles. The speed of the craft was varied and ranged from a cruising speed of thirty m.p.h. to great velocity. Their passage through our skies was frequently described as the sailing of a boat (rather majestically) or as the rising and falling of a bird in flight. Some of the craft put on quite a display while dipping from two thousand feet to one thousand feet and circling around.

"In one instance, two local residents of Gore (South Island) reported having seen, at night, a boat-shaped object carrying two large fans and three lights—which at times were covered by the fans. Two other residents (dredge hands) in the same locality reported an object shaped like a boat with an open top that came down through the mist in the early morning. The dredge hands swear they could discern two figures on board the craft. A similar airship was seen by several schoolchildren at noon. They stated it had the figure of a man seated in it. The manager of a firm in Dargaville observed a cigar-shaped object which moved along the coast, five miles from the shore. He watched it for fifteen minutes while it sailed on majestically. . . .

"There is no evidence to suggest that the year 1909 produced any UFO landings in New Zealand. To most witnesses the six-week flurry of sightings was, however, convincing enough to accept that intelligently controlled alien craft of an unknown identity had been visiting New Zealand skies. . . ."

If we take all these three major cigar waves of 1896–97 in the United States, and 1909 in both Britain and New Zealand, into account, we are faced with the very probable fact that some alien intelligence was taking a good, hard look at us. The interesting point is that they seemed only to manifest in cigar-shaped objects, which at night turned on powerful searchlights. What was the reason for these three remarkable cigar flaps in three scattered parts of the world?

We will be advancing some possible theories for these earlier appearances of cigar-shaped UFOs a little further on. However, we must next take a look at another odd phenomenon which took place in the thirties.

17

The Mystery Airplanes

Hardly had the mystery airship flaps of 1909 finished when we started to be plagued with "phantom" airplanes.

John A. Keel's article "Mystery Airplanes of the 1930s" was serialized in *Flying Saucer Review*. Actually Mr. Keel stated that this phase in UFO history started in 1910 when one of the earliest known aircraft in this category performed at night, hazardous manoeuveres at treetop level over New York City in that year.[56]

Keel wrote: "According to the New York *Tribune* of August 31, 1910, it was heard before it was seen. The whirring sound of a motor high in the air caused many necks to be craned toward the Metropolitan tower at 8:45 o'clock when a long black object was seen flying through the air toward the tower. The vague bulk, as it came into nearer view, took on the semblance of a biplane. It swung past the tower, then turned and described one graceful circle after another around the illuminated structure, its outlines standing out clear in the lights from many windows."

The very next night the airplane came back and repeated the same performance. The *Tribune* concluded that none of the known pilots in the vicinity were responsible. Indeed, Keel states, the "primitive open biplanes of that day could hardly risk fighting the dangerous updrafts around Manhattan's towers and few pilots were willing to attempt night flying at all."

Although Keel reports that there were a few other mysterious aviators from 1910 onward, it was in the Thirties that the "ghost" fliers really got around.

"One of the first ghost flier reports to appear in *Dagens-Nyheter* (Stockholm) in 1933, came from Kalix on December 24, 1933. It stated simply: 'A mysterious aeroplane appeared from the direction of the Bottensea at about 6:00 P.M. Christmas Eve, passed over Kalix, and continued westward. Beams of light came from the machine, searching the area.' "

Now, these beams of light are very interesting. Keel comments that they are a regular feature of modern UFO phenomena. We have seen, too, that they were a frequent characteristic of the airship flaps of 1896–97 and 1909, taking the form of what we now term searchlights. Keel makes the interesting observation that in 1934 our planes were equipped with landing lights similar to automobile headlights, and that these would not have been sufficient to provide the powerful lights beamed from the "ghost" fliers.

Keel points out that these fantastic "ghost" aviators were capable of flying in impossibly difficult weather conditions. He quotes a story from the *New York Times* about an aircraft flying over New York in a heavy snowstorm on December 26, 1933.

According to Keel, "The plane was first heard circling above Park Avenue and Twenty-second Street at 9:30 A.M. Numerous witnesses began to call the National Broadcasting Company. Reports continued until 2:25 P.M., meaning that the mystery plane had circled over Manhattan in a blinding snowstorm for five full hours. An amazing endurance feat, if nothing else."

Keel reported that in Scandinavia the "ghost" fliers were very active, and that "35 percent of all the known sightings of the 1934 Scandinavian wave took place during severe weather conditions. Heavy snowstorms, blizzards, and dense fog were mentioned in many of the accounts. The aircraft even operated at very low level during snowstorms, hedge-hopping with great skill and circling low over villages, ships, and railway stations in hazardous mountain regions remarkably similar to the rugged terrain around Cody, Wyoming."

Apparently, the governments of Sweden, Norway, and Denmark took the ghost flier reports very seriously and launched massive investigations. Keel states: "On April 30, 1934, Major General Reutersward, commanding general of Upper Norrland, made this statement to the press: 'Comparisons of these reports show that there can be no doubt about illegal air traffic over our secret military areas. There are many reports from reliable people which describe close observations of the enigmatic flier. And in every case the same remark can be noted: no insignia or identifying marks were visible on the machines. . . .' It is impossible to explain away the whole thing as mere imagination. The question is: Who or what are they, and why have they been invading our territory?"

Hundreds of reports continued to be turned in. For instance, the *New York Times* stated: "January 11, 1934, Alvkarleby. The ghost flier is still mocking his pursuers and seems to be growing bolder. At the moment there are reports about a greyish aircraft from Alvkarleby.

"An observation of the ghost flier over the forts of Boden caused a sensation. A military guard also saw him over other nearby forts.

"The Minister of Defense, Vennerstrom, was informed about the incident, but after a telephone conference with the military commander in Boden he denied the rumor.

" 'We are dealing with more than one machine,' General Virgin said. 'There's no doubt about it.'

"Military headquarters refused to say anything further on the matter."

Now, what were these "phantom" aviators doing flying over New York and Scandinavia, mostly in terrible weather conditions to which they seemed impervious, at the same time showing tremendous skill and beaming down powerful lights to enable them to search the area they were operating over?

Very similar questions arise in regard to the "ghost" fliers of the thirties. The only difference this time is that the vehicle is an airplane.

However, another very significant factor is becoming increasingly obvious. The manner in which these "ghost" fliers operate quite imperturbably in blizzards and snowstorms seems to indicate that they are from another dimension or space-time continuum. Our weather was not affecting them in the slightest.

18

The Mystery Rockets

In Chapter One we briefly mentioned the mystery "ghost" rockets that appeared over Scandinavia in 1946.

The French newspaper *Le Figaro* reported:

"More than two thousand ghost rockets have been reported during the past few months over Sweden. . . . They are the subject of jokes on the music-hall stage, but the Swedish and Danish military staffs are taking the matter seriously, and have begun an investigation. . . ."[57]

There were numerous references to these sightings in Scandinavian papers. At first there was some speculation that they might have been of Russian origin, but this soon was discounted.

Bjorn Overbye, one of Norway's regular *Flying Saucer Review* correspondents, in an article in that magazine called "Ghost-Bombs over Sweden," stated: "But why should anyone have been interested in dispatching secret weapons over Sweden? Better to have gone to a deserted place to test them. In addition one might ask who was capable of making such weapons at that time? The German experts had fled to the U.S.A., and those few who had been captured by the Russians were known not to be capable of making such weapons, a fact known to the Swedish army."[58]

Overbye went on to quote from the *Aftenposten* of July 17, 1946, "A large number of rockets have been observed during the last few days. They have been seen all over Scandinavia, and even from Finland we have received stories about objects moving with tremendous speed in the night skies. It is now believed that they are rockets constructed on entirely new principles."

However, *Le Figaro* in its story of September 5 reported that the ghost rockets did not by any means always travel at such tremendous speeds. The newspaper stated: "(1) The projectiles are in the shape of cigars. (2) Flames are projected out of their tail. The color is orange, but some people have said they were green. (3) They travel at an altitude of three hundred to one thousand meters. (4) Their speed is about that of an airplane. Some say a rather slow airplane. . . . (5) They do not make any noise, except a slight whistling."

For instance, Overbye gives us this example (July, Norland): "A silvery-colored torpedo was seen in the sky. It moved at an almost uncanny slow speed, and its altitude of flight was very low. After a time it disappeared behind some clouds."

After giving some more reports, Overbye wrote, "The Army, having made a semiofficial investigation during July, promised at the beginning of August to produce a report on the observations. This report never materialized, possibly because of so-called national security; or perhaps the investigation led to results that they did not dare publish either for fear of not being believed or of creating mass hysteria. The theory that the objects were comets or asteroids had been rejected by so many scientists that it was no longer of interest. All that remained was wild speculation mingled with the feeling that these things were not of earthly origin."

A large number of the objects seen over Scandinavia were not nearly so large as those observed in the earlier "flaps" described in the last few chapters over the United States, Britain, and New Zealand. In fact, a lot of them were only about ten feet in length. Possibly they were remote-controlled objects sent out by some bigger mother ships located at a much higher altitude in the earth's atmosphere. This, of course, is pure conjecture.

For instance, the *Dagens Nyheter* reported on August 9: "Laxa. At 8:00 P.M. six persons saw an object passing over the rooftops. It was shaped like a nine-foot-long cigar and at the nose we could see some small spheres; a bluish light was produced at the rear. No sound was heard."

The last report came at the end of August. Then, there were no more "ghost rockets." As suddenly as they came, they departed.

However, we should not close this chapter without mentioning that the modern UFO era had already begun at the beginning of that month in the U.S., and this also involved a cigar-shaped object.

At about 6:00 P.M. on August 1, 1946, Captain Jack E. Puckett was flying a C-47 plane from Langley Field, Virginia, to MacDill Field, Florida.[59]

The aircraft was at four thousand feet and about thirty miles northeast of Tampa when Captain Puckett and his crew were startled to see a cigar-shaped object hurtling toward them in horizontal flight at the same altitude.

When the cigar was about a thousand yards distant it swerved to avoid them and as the UFO passed them the crew could see that the object was twice the size of a B-29 bomber and had luminous portholes.

In addition to Captain Puckett, both his co-pilot, Lieutenant Henry, and his engineer witnessed the object. When they landed a full report was given to the Base Operations Section of MacDill Field. A signed report of Captain Puckett's remarkable sighting is on file at the National Investigations Committee on Aerial Phenomena headquarters. For some extraordinary reason, this important incident is not mentioned in the copious Condon Report!

Once again, we ask the same question. What was the purpose of this sustained demonstration of cigar-shaped objects over Scandinavia in 1946?

19

The Mystery Progression

The following year, 1947, saw the modern UFO phenomena erupt in the United States. From then on, an enormous variety of UFOs materialized in all conceivable shapes and sizes everywhere on earth (see Appendix).

Now, possibly you will have noticed something.

(1) The cigar flaps of 1896–97 and 1909 in the United States, the United Kingdom, and New Zealand occurred at a time when we were just starting to develop airships.

(2) The mystery airplanes of the thirties were around—actually, according to Keel, since 1910—at a time when our concentration was on developing aircraft. The thirties saw many wonderful pioneer record-breaking flights. Remember Amy and Jim Mollison?

(3) The mystery rockets in 1946 came just after we had let off the atom bomb, and we had now gotten the basic nuclear physics which would pave the way for our venture into space. We had, of course, been experimenting with rockets for some time, and it was rocketry that was to provide the impetus—the thrust—to get our spaceships into outer space in the years ahead.

(4) Then came the UFOs in their infinite variety of shapes and sizes. Perhaps to show us that we do not have to rely on the expensive rocketry, once we had graduated. If we could overcome what is called gravity, then maybe we could put up almost anything. In any case, that is what we were seeing up in our skies, UFOs of almost every possible shape and size.

The main point about all this is that there appears to have been some form of progression. The airship, the airplane, the rocket, and then the spaceship. Possibly we have some slender clue here.

Now, let us explore two possible theories.

(1) First, let us look at the idea that the Sky People are trying to encourage us to get a high degree of technology through our own efforts, but occasionally giving us a "shot in the arm," maybe unobtrusively, and at the same time certainly in the last few decades by giving us demonstrations.

I could be wide of the mark, but an incident connected with the legendary Comte de St.-Germain, whom Frederick the Great referred to as "the man who does not die" comes to mind.

According to Madame de Pompadour, the Comte claimed to possess the secret of eternal youth. He always looked about forty or forty-five years old. Many people claimed to have seen him in their old age looking exactly the same as when they met him in their own forties! A brilliant linguist, St.-Germain spoke German, English, Italian, Portuguese, Spanish, Greek, Latin, Sanskrit, Arabic, and Chinese, besides being a great musician and an excellent chemist (that is, an alchemist).

Anyway, Franz Graeffer, in his *Recollections of Vienna,* recounts the following incident in the life of the astonishing Comte:

"St.-Germain then gradually passed into a solemn mood. For a few seconds he became as rigid as a statue; his eyes, which were always expressive beyond words, became dull and colorless. Presently, however, his whole being became reanimated. He made a movement with his hand as if in signal of departure, then said 'I am leaving *(Ich scheide),* do not see me. Once again will you see me. Tomorrow night I am off; I am much needed in Constantinople, then in England, *there to prepare two inventions which you will have in the next century —trains and steamboats.*' "[60] (Italics mine.)

This event happened in the eighteenth century. Although the steam engine was really invented by James Watt in the eighteenth century, the first successful steam engine on railways was George Stephenson's *Rocket* in 1829.

The first practical steamboat was the tug *Charlotte Dundas,* built by William Symington, and tried in the Forth and Clyde Canal in 1802.[61]

St.-Germain could well have been a spaceman living among us. This, I realize, is wild speculation. However, his long, almost immortal life has been well authenticated.

It is a well-known fact that when the time is ripe a new invention arrives. Often it is discovered at almost the same moment by more than one person working independently in entirely different parts of the world. It is "in the air," so to speak.

Why is it in the air? Perhaps, at different times, when the time is ripe, these ideas have been "planted" by people like St.-Germain.

Could the mystery airships have been demonstrated in the skies over the United States, Britain, and New Zealand to show what could be achieved in this direction "upstairs"?

It is pretty interesting to note that these early cigar flaps pretty well coincided with our first efforts to get into the air at all, and, of course, the modern UFO phenomena with our own initial steps into space. Maybe, we are being assisted behind the scenes more than the public realizes.

I realize that some readers may think that all this is a very naïve suggestion, but some of you may think it has possibilities.

Now we will take a look at my second possibility.

(2) If you are "off-planet," that is, on a planet far off in our galaxy, or perhaps, in one of those invisible universes we have been talking about, then if you were one of "them," you would try to disguise yourself if you were making a reconnaissance of our planet for some purposes you wanted to keep to yourself.

Therefore, in 1896–97, and in 1909, you would think, "They are now exploring the possibility of airships and some of them have gotten off the ground in a primitive way." So, you appear in airships to do your reconnaissance, hoping that the people will think your ships are their own, or be written off as delusions. You appear over the United States in 1896–97, where you are helped by hoaxes and phony write-ups by journalists. In 1909 you appear over Britain in the early part of the year, and in the second portion over the skies of New Zealand. Then, in the thirties you copy our planes and, since you are able to fly extradimensionally, the blizzards do not affect your craft in the slightest degree. Finally, you produce your "ghost rockets" over Scandinavia, and now we have your craft in all shapes and sizes cavorting around the air space of our world. Some people, including many eminent UFO writers and researchers, seem to fear you and feel that you are planning a take-over of our planet.

Well, there it is. Two theories. Maybe both are wrong and the answer lies in another direction. However, they may stimulate the thought processes.

20

The Mystery
of the Faceless Woman

The UFO story is not a clear-cut one of visitors coming here from outer space. There are many mysterious facets to the subject—"wheels within wheels."

In the first part of this book the mystery of why the UFOs are the best kept secret in the world was discussed. In the second part a very strong connection with the paranormal was indicated. Now, in this third section, a possible link—even a progression—between the early mystery airships, the phantom fliers of the thirties, and the ghost rockets of 1946, leading up to modern UFO phenomena, has been suggested.

Additionally, some very strange experiences have occurred to people all over the world during recent years. It is becoming increasingly obvious that the ufonauts come from many areas. It is possible that some emanate from outer space. Some from invisible universes, or other space-time continuums. Some of the visitors may be benevolent, others indifferent, and some downright hostile.

If we bear all this in mind then it will come as no surprise to learn of the very odd experiences two reputable ladies went through recently in Ohio.[62] These two extraordinary contact stories are more bizarre than anything else related so far in this book. However, they are included here because this type of contact is becoming increasingly commonplace. John A. Keel in *UFOs: Operation Trojan Horse* has reported a considerable number of odd happenings of this nature. It therefore deserves careful study and is one of those mysterious facets mentioned earlier. One of the many "wheels within wheels."

During the last two weeks of July and the first two weeks of August 1969, there were scattered reports in Ohio of TV interference. Black and white sets were giving colors, and color TV sets were showing fantastic colors never seen before. Voices were heard that did not come from the programs being observed. During this identical period many UFOs were reported over the same area.

Then, the first Monday in August, a woman from the West Hill district, Mrs. Dollie Hansen, of Westward, West Akron, telephoned Mrs. Madeline Teagle, chairman of Contact (U.S.A.), which is part of a worldwide UFO organization, stating she was in touch with the occupants of a UFO and expected to be taken for a trip the coming Thursday.

Mrs. Teagle asked her to call back after completing the voyage. Mrs. Hansen was also requested to ask her hosts to pick up a few other individuals who wanted to go on a journey in a spaceship, a little boy and two other people.

Mrs. Hansen called back on Friday morning. Prior to her call, Contact (U.S.A.) had a report from one of her neighbors to the effect that at about 2:00 A.M. they had been awakened by a fantastic brilliant flash, and on looking out of the window observed that the house across the street (which belonged to Mrs. Hansen) was lit up with a blinding white light. It was so brilliant that every detail of the house was to be clearly seen.

Their first thought was that an explosion had taken place. Then, when the witnesses heard no noise, and as the light remained constant and steady, they began to think there was something very strange going on. That is why they telephoned Mrs. Teagle the next day to tell her about this odd business, knowing that she would be interested and that it might be connected with the UFOs.

Mrs. Hansen had a most extraordinary story to relate over the telephone on the Friday morning.

At around midnight her entire family was soundly asleep,

but she remained up until about 2:00 A.M., when a knock came at her door. Outside was a superbly built young woman with "the most beautiful dark chestnut, almost black hair I have ever seen anywhere. The hair was so lustrous and unusual that I would recall it anywhere if I saw it again."

However, this unusually beautiful girl had no features where her face should have been. Nonetheless, the young woman of earth had no fear and went directly with her visitor.

Outside, a black car waited. In it were two men, in the front seat. Where the dashboard usually is located was a large red box. Mrs. Hansen had the impression that this was used to communicate with the spaceship.

As soon as the car moved off, *a gray or black mist began to envelop the car, both inside and out.* The reason for this, her escort explained, was to make sure that no one saw them leave, and that their guest could not see in what direction she was being taken.

(Please note certain similarities here to the case of the Japanese bank manager and his friends who suddenly saw the car ahead of them encircled by a white mist and disappear. Incidentally, could the black car ahead have contained an alien? See Chapter Seven.)

The spaceship was waiting for them in a clearing in some woods. Mrs. Hansen remembered that they had to walk across some spongy, marshy ground to reach the ship. The steps for boarding seemed to materialize right out of the craft and then to melt into it again.

There were no visible seams or welds anywhere. The interior was softly lighted.

At about 2:30 A.M., the ship picked up a little crippled boy in East Akron, and two more people from other nearby locations. These were the people that Mrs. Teagle had asked to be taken for rides, if it was possible.

Shortly, after Mrs. Hansen had called up to give her account, the little boy telephoned. He said that *on the Thursday night there was a strong impression that a UFO was going to take him for a ride.*

Therefore, he had bathed, dressed in clean new pajamas, and sat on the couch until around 2:30 A.M., when sleep came to him. He was still there upon awakening around ten the following morning.

Two weeks after this remarkable incident, another woman, Mrs. Joyce Vellacca, of Killian Road, South Akron, telephoned Contact (U.S.A.) to say that she and her husband had been out for a hamburger the previous night and spotted a large, orange red ball of light in the south east sky, near Goodyear Aerospace. It did not change size, position, or shape, but did seem to pulsate from red to orange through to white and back again in that color order.

When they returned home and had put the car away, the object was still to be seen in the sky. They stood outside their house to see what would happen to the UFO. By this time they had determined it was not an airplane or any ordinary source of light.

Mrs. Vellacca stated they first noted it at precisely 12:20 A.M., and at exactly 1:30 A.M. "it simply went out."

("It simply went out." Another example of dematerialization. See Chapter Nine.)

Mr. and Mrs. Vellacca went inside their house, but were both so keyed up as a result of their sighting that they could not go to bed and sat up talking till 4:00 A.M. Then, Mr. Vellacca elected to try to get a little sleep.

His wife decided to lie down on the sofa for a few winks. However, she had scarcely stretched out when a big gust of wind swept through the window and blew the curtains out. She jumped up to close the window and froze in her tracks. Mrs. Vellacca stated that she was unable to move. Literally, paralyzed to the spot.

And . . . standing on the other side of the window, looking back at her, was a woman, marvelously built, with the most beautiful long dark chestnut, almost black hair she had ever seen. "If I ever see that head of hair anywhere," she commented, "I will know who it belongs to, for I have never seen hair such as that on any mortal."

But the woman had no discernible features where her face would be located.

Oddly enough, when Mrs. Vellacca recovered from her frozen immobility, the visitor had gone. She rushed outside and turned on all the floodlights to illuminate the area, but could see nothing unusual. Then there came a high-pitched whine similar to that of a motorcycle, except that when that machine reaches its take-off there is a loud roar. This was not audible. Instead, the noise gained in shrill frequency until it was no longer heard. The dogs in the neighborhood were raising a great rumpus.

Shortly afterward, Mrs. Teagle and other members of Contact (U.S.A.) visited the area and inspected the ground behind Mr. and Mrs. Vellacca's home. There is a small wood bordering the Firestone Golf Course. Next to this wood, there is a weed field and then their house.

The woods, Mrs. Teagle reports, match perfectly the drawing subsequently made by Mrs. Dollie Hansen of the spot she was driven to in the black car to board the UFO. Right down to the tall blue spruce, a border of which she thought to be barberry but which were in fact blueberry bushes, which has a very similar leaf. The same spongy marshy ground over which she had to walk to the ship.

Well, here is certainly another mystery. What was the purpose of the two contacts? Why did the second one in some way misfire? Why did the lady with the beautiful hair have no facial features? Was she possibly wearing some kind of mask? Is there some kind of lesson to be learned from this?

Other faceless encounters are occurring. This is a new phase in the flying-saucer saga, something for us to ponder over. There surely must be a reason for these very strange events.

Many encounters have been made with what have come to be termed "humanoids." These are usually rather small beings dressed in what appear to be one-piece "spacesuits." Often, they are found taking samples of our fauna and, if discovered by earth people, take off into the blue quickly. It is possible that they are robotlike beings working for a superior race.

On the other hand, when the real entities appear, whether they are "goodies" or "baddies," perhaps, they are careful to disguise themselves to some extent.

Anyway, we have much to sort out here. The flying-saucer saga is not all plain sailing. There are certain guidelines, but there are wide areas still be explored.

21

The Mystery of the UFO Emblem

Some of the most authentic and extraordinary photographs of a UFO were taken on June 1, 1967, at San José de Valderas, near Madrid, Spain.

Señor Antonio Ribera, Spain's foremost ufologist, wrote in *Flying Saucer Review:*

"San José de Valderas is one of those ultra-modern housing settlements, consisting of large blocks of flats, that have sprung up around Madrid in step with this capital's excessive expansion. It so happens by a lucky chance that at San José de Valderas and near the Extremadura highway there are a few rural belts with meadows and copses of woodland. It was in one of these areas, dominated by the silhouette of the ancient castle of the Marqués de Valderas (used at the present time to house a college run by nuns of the Orden del Amor de Díos) that several people were enjoying the fresh evening air at sundown on June 1, or were resting or reading their papers, when they suddenly saw a strange disc-shaped object which appeared almost immediately over the castle and then performed revolutions over the area for a period of some twelve minutes, flying so low that it almost grazed the tops of the trees, fluttering to and fro in a strange movement like a falling dead leaf, and finally vanishing in the direction of the Extremadura highway. The object appeared to correspond to the classic descriptions of "flying saucers." It was perfectly round, about twelve or thirteen meters wide, and seemed to consist of two washbasins placed with their concave sides facing each other. On the under part, the belly of the craft bore a curious sign—very similar to the sign on the UFO seen at Aluche [this was on February 6, 1966, in the Madrid suburb of Aluche] but with the parallel lines (the center one being shorter) linked by another horizontal line. . . ."[63]

The UFO was not only seen by scores of witnesses but photographed by at least two of them.

After the UFO flew off along the Extremadura highway—where it was seen by numerous other witnesses, including an engineer—the object "landed for a few moments on an open piece of ground in the suburb of Santa Monica, some four kilometers, as the crow flies from San José de Valderas. It landed close to the restaurant known by the name of 'La Ponderosa.' The owner of this restaurant is Señor Antonio Muñoz, who at that precise moment was perched on a stepladder and stringing up colored lightbulbs around the patio, while his chef was helping by holding the ladder. Suddenly, a lot of very excited people began streaming onto the patio, all declaring the same thing: namely, that they had seen a ball of fire, of enormous size, which in the cases of several of them passed right above their very heads and was lowering three 'legs' to make a landing."

Then, Ribera remarks, "we come to one of the most baffling aspects of this whole affair." Some mysterious metal tubes were found at the landing site.

One of these tubes was picked up by a young boy who had found it by chance, and had opened it with a pair of pliers. The boy said that when he opened the tube a liquid had escaped from it and evaporated.

Now, here is something extremely interesting. Ribera states, *"The tube contained two green strips, apparently of plastic, bearing a curious embossed emblem reminiscent of the mark on the belly of the UFO."* (Italics mine.)

These strips and a piece of the metal tube were eventually sent to the laboratories of the INTA (the Spanish National

Technical Institute for Aeronautics and Space Research) in Madrid.

Ribera commented, "The INTA analyzed them, and sent us a very detailed report on their findings: the metal sample was nickel of an extraordinarily high degree of purity, while the plastic strip was polyvinyl fluoride, a type of plastic not yet available commercially. Consulting the technical literature on the subject, we discovered that this material, up to that date had been manufactured by the American firm of Dupont de Nemours. It had been made in a pilot plant by them for the American National Aeronautical and Space Administration (NASA). The latter were using it as a facing for the cones of earth satellites, in order to protect them against the severe effects of the atmosphere, this plastic possessing extraordinary properties and being virtually everlasting and immune against damage by any corrosive agency."

Now, all this is highly suspicious. In an earlier book, *The Flying Saucer Story,* I gave an account of the Socorro landing in 1964. Briefly, at about 5:30 P.M., on April 24 of that year, Lonnie Zamora, a Socorro, New Mexico, police officer, was in his patrol car, and came in contact with what at first he thought was an overturned car. However, upon arriving at the spot he found an egg-shaped object with markings over a foot high in red on one side of the craft.[64]

This particular sighting was investigated by Dr. J. Allen Hynek, then civilian consultant to the now defunct Project Blue Book, and it is regarded as not only a classic sighting but a baffling one. However, the point I want to make is that the markings reproduced in my earlier book and which have appeared elsewhere *are not the true ones.* I understand that the Central Intelligence Agency (CIA) stepped in very quickly and deliberately altered the markings. Furthermore, a book will be published shortly written by a ufologist who was with Dr. Hynek at the investigation, setting the record straight. However, I am told that the original markings on the Socorro object are not the same as on the San José de Valderas UFO.

Now, when you take into account that as far as we are

aware, out of all the thousands of UFOs reported, the only ones known to have had markings on them are the UFOs at Aluche and San José de Valderas in Spain, and the Socorro object in New Mexico, then a certain line of thought comes into operation.

The question arises: Are these particular ones man-made? If they are made by the Americans, then it is very likely that they would put some form of marking on them.

The fact too, that the type of plastic used in the tubes found on the ground is being used by NASA in the cones of earth satellites is very suspicious.

It is a well-known fact that the American aircraft companies have been trying to solve the gravity problem for years. Something like sixteen years ago, Derek D. Dempster, who was then aviation correspondent of the London *Daily Express,* and also the first editor of *Flying Saucer Review,* wrote in the January-February 1956 issue of the magazine:[65]

"The great puzzle now is: 'How much information has been gleaned from the prize apparently in the possession of the U.S., and is it the reason for the sudden and intense activity now associated with gravity research?' "

(Mr. Dempster had been commenting on the possibility that the U.S. authorities had a landed UFO in their possession.)

"The answer is a very difficult one to give at this juncture, but a brief review of the activities now going on in America may help to point to a conclusion. Last autumn it was disclosed that no less than thirty-five electronics and aeronautics companies and a number of universities and foundations were working on a program designed to probe the secrets of gravity under the direction of some of America's top scientists. In addition, one of the aviation firms—the Martin Aircraft Company—had signed on two of Europe's leading authorities on gravity and electromagnetism: Dr. Burkhard Heim, Professor of Theoretical Physics at Goettingen University, and Dr. Pascual Jordan of Hamburg University.

"Centers where pure research on gravity is now in progress

in some form or another include the Institute for Advanced Study at Princeton, New Jersey, and Princeton University; the University of Indiana's School of Advanced Mathematical Study, and the Purdue University Research Foundation."

Mr. Dempster went on to list aircraft companies and other scientists interested at that time in gravity research. If all that work was going on some sixteen years ago, very considerable advances must have been achieved in this field since then.

The Americans could have reached the stage where they have top-secret experimental "flying saucers." A recent article in Ray Palmer's *Flying Saucers,* an American UFO magazine, lists a remarkable number of patents granted by the United States patent office over the last few years, all of which are for inventions necessary for manufacturing a flying saucer![66]

The day will come when the United States authorities announce to the world that the flying saucers do exist and that they are man-made by them.

When that day comes, ufologists must be prepared to deal with an even more complex situation. It will be hard to spot the real UFOs from elsewhere when man-made saucers are flying openly around.

Meanwhile, we can wonder about the markings on the UFOs seen in Spain. Were those particular UFOs secret American experimental craft?

On the other hand, Antonio Ribera and his associates are following up another fascinating trail. When Señor Ribera has collected sufficient evidence regarding his investigations, he will, possibly, publicize the results.[67]

Whatever the answer to the mystery of the markings on the UFOs seen in Spain, you have been warned. It is very possible that the United States government may announce this year, next year, or in the foreseeable future that the elusive flying saucers are made by them. Some of the UFOs may now be man-made, but do not be fooled. They are not all man-made. Not by any means.

Plate 12: UFO over San Jose de Valderas, Spain, seen in horizontal flight

Plate 13: The same UFO tilted so that the strange marking is clearly visible on the under part

Plate 14: Flying saucers over a town. This imaginative drawing illustrates some of the shapes of UFO's seen during the last twenty-five years (see Appendix A). Photo courtesy of *Kiril Tirzier*.

Plate 15: UFO over McMinnville, Oregon. Photographed by *Paul Trent* on May 11, 1950.

Plate 16: Photograph of "angel hair"

Plate 17: UFO sighted over Pennsylvania

Plate 18: Doughnut-shaped UFO

SECOND INTERLUDE

22

What Is It All About?

An imaginary conversation between a reader and the author:

Reader: Your book is all very disturbing. What is this UFO business all about? What are they doing here invading our air space? Who are they, anyway? I understand there have been hundreds of reported landings. Why don't they ask permission to land? They are infringing both our national and international laws.

Author: Neither did we ask permission to land on the moon.

Reader: Actually, I have read in other books of ufonauts taking samples of water from our lakes and stealing plants. You state they have taken our animals, as well as some human beings.

Author: Yes. However, won't we do the same? We have already brought back rock samples from the moon. No doubt, if we find some animals on one of the planets, we will pinch a few of the equivalent of their steers and sheep, or whatever they have. When we do bring them back, no doubt our experts will look them over, and they will end their days in our zoos. Maybe we'll catch one or two of the natives, too, and bring them in for questioning.

Reader: Yes, but these entities that appear to people. They seem so varied. Such extraordinary sizes. Some are eleven feet tall and others only three feet in height, or less.

Author: On our planet there are people of varying sizes.

Some by our standards are very tall, and then, in Africa, there are pygmies of very small stature. So, from elsewhere, we must expect similar differences in size. You must also take into account the amount of gravity on a planet. This influences the growth of both plant and animal life. In fact, as the visitors may be coming from not only our whole physical universe containing billions of star systems, but possibly from invisible universes as well, it is more than likely that some of them may be taller than our own species, and some smaller. After all, there is evidence that in antedeluvian times there were giants on the earth.

Reader: Yes, that sounds feasible. But, I don't like the way they are all over the place now. Why are they taking such an intense interest in us at this time?

Author: Well, there are records that they have always been around all through history.

It is true that since the end of the last world war they have increased their visits. This is only speculation, but they may have reasoned since we let the bomb off that our first ventures into space would follow soon afterward, since nuclear fission gave us the key. Therefore, they decided to watch earth people more closely. After all, up till then we had been content to coast along for hundreds of years without much of a technology.

Reader: I'm not sure if I go along with that theory. It all looks like a great build-up to an invasion or take-over of our planet. Did I not read in an earlier book of yours that there were some entities around the earth who are hostile to us?

Author: Yes, there are known to be some who are not exactly friendly. They are alleged to come from an invisible area. Several other ufologists have advanced this view in books and magazine articles. However, these unpleasant entities are not the real Sky People.

Reader: The extrasensory powers that ufonauts possess seem rather frightening. I mean levitating, materializing and dematerializing, and the ability to walk through walls, that sort of thing. In any case, it does seem rather hard to swallow.

Author: I did mention the early saints. The Vatican has some pretty authentic records, you know. Don't forget, too, that there are a number of yogis in Tibet and other places credited with some quite remarkable feats of this nature.

Humanity has regarded itself as the apex of all being for so long that it comes as rather a shock to learn that there could be an alien race not only capable of having had space travel for millennia, but also able to perform extra sensory feats such as you have mentioned, as a normal way of life.

Actually, it is all a matter of understanding. If you understand the laws of life and the way in which things are done, then you are at ease. There is no fear. It is like the first time you try to ride a bicycle. You probably fall off. Possibly you are afraid of it for a time. Certainly you are not at ease in regard to riding it. Then you learn how to balance yourself on the bicycle and your fear goes.

Reader: I see what you mean. However, are you sure the UFO people are not planning to invade us?

Author: It is my contention that they put us here originally, and literally seeded us. So obviously they would have a very special interest in us. It is very likely that they have been watching over their product every since, judging by the reports of UFOs down the centuries. In a way, we have been in quarantine. You see, when humanity was made, it was an unknown quantity. The Makers did not know for certain how the result would turn out.

Reader: Makers? I always thought that God made our world, but you are talking of the Makers. What do you mean?

Author: Read the next few chapters in the book. They contain a concept which you must weigh and judge for yourself.

Of course, there is a Supreme Being, God, above all others. However, the manufacture of our physical universe, including this world and humanity, came about through— but you had better read it for yourself.

PART FOUR

A Cosmic Concept

23

The Manufacture of the Microcosm

We are going to put forward here a concept which is possibly outrageous and may run against a lot of accepted ideas and prejudices. This, of course, always happens with any new concepts that are on a collision course with accepted thought. However, we are not asking you to necessarily accept these ideas in their entirety, but to give them a little house room in the recesses of your mind. Treat the whole of this section, if you like, as pure speculation.

Broadly speaking, this concept goes right back to source. It does not just deal with the origins of mankind on this little mudball in space, but embraces the beginnings of our whole physical universe, as well as all the invisible ones, too. In short, the whole complete omniverse. It is a pretty ambitious concept. Mind-stretching in its cosmic approach.

Please remember that we are not trying to ram these ideas down anyone's throat. We admit a little bias toward them. Naturally, anyone producing such a cosmology is inclined in its favor. The reason for including this concept here is that it has a great bearing on the "Eternal Subject"—the continuous visitations of people from other realms to our planet.

Now, as stated earlier, we must go back to original source. In short, we must go back to God. At this stage, some of you will ask in exasperation, Why must we bring in such matters? The plain answer is that it has a lot to do with our case. Some of us believe and know that there is a God, call Him, Her, or

It, what you will: Almighty God, Great Architect, Principle, Original Primal Energy, or whatever. In this dissertation we will use the term "the Creator."

For a start we will postulate that the Creator created Man and nothing else! We are not talking here about humans, but real Man. These Men have been called and are the Sons of God. They were created perfect in spirit form or, if you like, as pure divine energy. They were capable of operating in Four Universes of Divine Mind. These Four Universes were those of Creative Mind, Analytical-Synthetic Mind, Emotion, and Form. So, you see that original Man was built on the Square. These four attributes embrace all the other subdivisions of mind.

The Sons of God, known in Hebrew literature as the Elohim, were capable of taking form and manifesting in any of these cosmic universes of mind. These Men were completely balanced in the use of their minds, unlike humans, who, generally speaking, live to a great extent on their emotions. Actually, humans are based chiefly in the emotional universe of Divine Mind and there is a reason for that, as we shall see later.

Now, these Sons of God were also capable of divine creation, which was their natural heritage, being who they were, the Sons of their Father. So, they followed in their Father's footsteps, as He would have wished, and used their inherent Creative abilities. They, in turn, created universes! They were not only Sons of God, but gods themselves, though respecting their Father as omniscient.

Of course, some bright person may ask who created God? We would suggest that He has always been present. However, there may be a continuous flow of Sons of God being created from various Fathers, and possibly, the Almighty God we commune with may not be the original one. We are on very controversial ground here! Indeed, we did state earlier that this was a mind-stretching exercise.

In my first book, *The Sky People,* it was suggested that

Jehovah, the God of the Old Testament, was one of the Elohim. In fact, that the Jehovah was not just one person but a race of gods. Furthermore, that the Jehovah, along with some of the other Elohim, had actually manufactured the chemical universe in which we live and have our being.

All real artists experiment and try to express themselves in different ways. Some brilliant ones have, at first, what appear to be failures. If we state here that the formation of the chemical universe and the subsequent manufacture of humanity was an initial failure, we do not mean to be discourteous or blasphemous to the Jehovah who formed it.

What we are writing here runs completely against all accepted beliefs. To recap, we are suggesting that the original Creator spawned in a spiritual manner Sons of God, capable of creating universes, too. That the Jehovah, a race of gods, part of the Elohim, formed the Chemical Universe we live in, and introduced the necessary particles to produce life. Subsequently, several attempts were made to manufacture intelligent life forms, as we will see in the next chapter.

We have already stated that the Elohim, the Sons of God, were capable of taking form in any of the Four Universes of Divine Mind. We are going to put forward our case that the Elohim formed the Chemical Universe (our own) inside the Cosmic Emotional Universe of Mind.

Another way of looking at what has been outlined here is to appreciate that the Four Cosmic Universes of Mind: the Creative, the Analytical-Synthetic, the Emotional, and the Formal, make up the Macrocosm; and our Chemical Universe, occupying part of the Macrocosmic Emotional Universe, is the Cosmic Microcosm.

The Four Original Universes are often referred to in symbolic literature—Alchemy, for instance—as Earth, Air, Fire and Water. Early scientific thought tried to find exact reproductions of them in the basic substance of the chemical world. The Emotional Universe from which the Chemical derived is called the element Water. Sometimes, it is referred to as the

Great Sea, and in this connection, chemical matter is relatively considered to be frozen out of it like ice. Although the analogy is not quite perfect, it will serve to promote a certain degree of understanding.

Every old religion, as we shall see, gives that creating race of gods who were made in the Cosmic Four, by the One True God, credit for organizing the Microcosm out of the Waters, or the Mother aspect of the Four Quarters of the Primordial Cosmos.

According to the priests of Heliopolis in Ancient Egypt, for example, the Primeval Four appeared in the Waters, one pair at a time, as the offspring and grandchildren of the First Spirit, the Creator, who became the High God by His act of Creation. Once the High God had established His Order and peopled it with Man, He withdrew Himself (or entered no further into the work of Creation). The Microcosm was then produced by the Four, personified as Shu and Tefnut, Geb and Nut. Nut was Sky of Space, and gave birth to five great children: Osiris and Isis, Seth and Nephtys, and the elder Horus.[68]

It is not difficult to see in all this the Four Cosmic elements at work, and it is particularly interesting to notice how, when the Microcosm is formed by the Great Mother, Nut, the scene of the drama shifts into it. The secondary influences of the Four, along with the Microcosm itself, become the five great children who were born to Nut "after she had given birth to the stars." All the rest of the story becomes a history of the secondary creation and of mankind's evolution within it.

The book of Genesis in our Bible does not give us such dramatic detail about the birth of the Microcosm, but nevertheless, the basic ingredient is there in the sentence, "The Spirit of God moved upon the face of the waters." The original text read "And the Spirit of the Elohim moved upon the face of the waters"!

In another book we referred to the Popul-Vuh, the sacred book of the Quiché-Maya. Its title means Book of the Community, or Book of the Council. It calls mankind (humanity) on Earth the "made man" and points out how he was made by a Cosmic Race of Man that came into being and had a long history of its own, before the chemical world was brought into existence. In fact it credits some of this cosmic race with the very fabrication of our chemical universe.[69]

The book opens with a description of the universe before the creation of material things or mankind. Like the book of Genesis, the story begins before the appearance of the earth and tells us there was only "calm sea" and the empty sky.

All was still, silent, and dark, except for the space immediately surrounding a group of Divine Beings. This area was illuminated by their shining. These Beings were resting in the Waters, and the Book enumerates them in pairs. There is considerable similarity here to the story already given from ancient Egypt. They were the Creator and the Maker, Tepeu and Gucumatz, the Four of highest rank. With them were E Alom (those who conceive and give birth), who are called the Forefathers, although one of them was thought of as being female, according to the system of arranging these causal Beings in male-female couples—a system as old as Egypt, Tibet and the earliest Hindu thought.

There was also present with these Beings a group of three others which the translator of the book associates with the Christian Triune God, and not unwisely. These three do the actual work of Creation under the supervision of Tepeu and Gucumatz, by command of the Creator and Maker. Tepeu and Gucumatz formulate the plans for Creation, but it is the Heart of Heaven, the three, who perform the actual function of making all earthly things and mankind.

The three personalities are Huracan, Chipi-Caculha and Rax-Caculha. All are associated through the meaning of their names with lightning and thunder (as the Hebrew Yaweh or Jehovah), and the name of the chief among them has been adapted into several languages to describe a violent type of tropical storm, the hurricane. They always work as a unit and the three together are often referred to by the name of the principle member, Huracan, who is called the Arranger.

After much meditation, discussion and long deliberation,

Tepeu and Gucumatz foresee the coming of dawn and the appearance of man. "Then they planned the creation," says the Popul-Vuh, "and Huracan, the Heart of Heaven, arranged it in the darkness and in the night." When all was prepared, Tepeu and Gucumatz spoke the commanding words and the earth began to appear from the surrounding waters.

The Tibetans, too, while recognizing and worshiping a Supreme Being—whom they call Vairochana—also, believed in the Macrocosm with its other universes, as well as a Microcosm. They, too, understood the Fourfold Cosmos and its many inhabitants.[70]

The Harranians and the Sumerians both taught that the Supreme God made the High Heavens (the Macrocosm, or Fourfold Cosmos) and that the Microcosm was made by some of His Sons, the inhabitants of the Macrocosm.[71] They recognized the Waters as a symbol of the source from which the Microcosm was made, and that is why they practiced baptism as a ritual of purification, and as a token of the eventual return of the lesser secondary creation to the Mother Universe (the Cosmic Emotional) from whose substance they were made. The practice of baptism has been carried on by Christians, too, although the original meaning has been partially lost.

We have described how all these people had in common the tradition of a Big Four, which played a very important part in the creation of this particular (chemical) universe. All these ancient peoples believed that *after* the Supreme God had created the Cosmos and peopled it with His Sons, that these Divine Beings (or, at any rate, some of them), in their turn, made the Chemical universe. This act in the ancient tradition was personified by Four Divine Beings, representing the Four Original Universes, or the Fourfold Cosmos.

We stated that the second verse of Chapter 1 of the book of Genesis (King James version) read, "And the Spirit of God moved upon the face of the waters." We were so bold as to remind you that in the older Hebrew translation the words read, "And the Spirit of the Elohim moved upon the face of the waters."

Now, this difference is all-important! In the Hebrew, the word Elohim means gods or divine beings. Do you see now that when rendered correctly, this account of the creation of the Chemical Universe ties in with those of the Quiché-Maya and of the Ancient Egyptians, each of whom described divine beings resting in the Waters?

We can say, therefore, that the ancient tradition of a Supreme Being—of the Fourfold Cosmos, the peopling of that Cosmos or Macrocosm with divine beings, and the subsequent making by these beings of a Microcosm inside one area of the Cosmos, the Waters or Matrix—is inherent in the most ancient traditions and religions of the world. It has survived down to our times, but it is literally buried beneath the stultifying blankets of misinterpretation, forgetfulness, and ignorance.

So far, we have concentrated to a great extent on the birth of the Microcosm (our chemical universe) within the Macrocosm. We will now give our attention to the advent of humanity.

24

The Manufacture of Humanity

There are many accounts to be found around the world in the religious books and legends of mankind as to how a Cosmic Race of gods from outside the Chemical Universe manufactured humanity.

We have described elsewhere how the first two chapters of Genesis contain two entirely separate creation stories. The first creation story refers to the establishment of the Golden Age—the creation of Galactic Man. "So God created man in his own image, in the image of God created he him: male and female created he them." (Genesis 1:27–28)

The second creation story in the next chapter of Genesis refers to the manufacture of humans with an earth-animal chemical body—the making of a *second Adam* by the Jehovah.

It is noticeable that in the second creation only Adam was made—doubtless not just one Adam but a race of humans. In the first creation both males and females were created. It is not till some time later in the second story that a mate was provided for Adam, through taking a rib from him. At least, that is what we are told in Genesis.

Erich von Daniken in his fascinating book *Return to the Stars,* writing on the creation accounts, suggests very sensibly —in the light of our present scientific knowledge—that Eve was produced in a retort.[72] However, he appears to have completely missed the point that the first two chapters of Genesis contain two entirely separate creation stories!

The Second Adam (humanity), animal man, was not originally intended by his Makers, the Jehovah, to be developed to a high estate. He was manufactured *to keep and to guard* the Garden of Eden. This is stated quite clearly in Genesis.

It would seem that some of the Sky People, known as the Dragon or Serpent People since time immemorial, may have visited the Garden out of curiosity to learn what was going on there, as it was guarded by these newly made humans. Dutifully, the humans no doubt turned them away. However, we can surmise that fraternization took place between the Serpent People and the human womenfolk. Probably, the Sky People took compassion on these primitive animal humans walking around naked and enlightened them on a few of the facts of life! When the Jehovah (Elohim) came round on their next tour of inspection they found Adam hiding in the brushwood wearing some kind of clothes.

The Jehovah asked point-blank:

"Who told thee that thou wast naked?" He was very angry. This exasperation occurred again when he cursed the Sky People for their interference. The rest you know. This was the so-called Fall. The humans were turned out of the Garden and taken back to the place from which they were originally taken —the planet earth. Tradition has it that an unholy row occurred between the race of Jehovah and some of the other Elohim who had not taken part in the manufacture of humanity, and that the Jehovah accompanied His human creation back to Earth.

The Popul-Vuh, the Sacred Book of the Quiché-Maya, described at least four attempts by the gods to manufacture suitable beings to serve and worship them. However, before these efforts they first made a race called U-vinaquil huyub— "the little man of the forest," but he was not human. He did not have a chemical-animal body. He was reminiscent of the elves, fairies, and gnomes of European folklore. These are still with us today.

Then, the gods tried to get the animals and birds to worship them, but they could not make words. This experiment failed. So, they tried again.

They set about producing "obedient respectful beings" to "nourish and sustain them." First, they tried to make a man out of mud, but the mud melted. It could speak a little, but could not reproduce itself.

They destroyed the mud-men and held another conference. They then decided to make men out of wood who would "nourish, sustain, invoke, and remember them." The new wooden creatures lived and multiplied, but were also a disappointment. They wandered about on all fours, had no soul, were mindless, and, worst of all, they had no memory. They too, failed to nourish, sustain, invoke, adore, or remember their makers, so the Heart of Heaven, Huracan, destroyed them all in a great flood.

In the Maya country there is a plant which produces a pod containing red seeds like beans. The Creator and the Maker decided to use these as materials in their next attempt to make humans. They proposed to make woman's flesh from rushes. However, this third type of man fared no better than his predecessors, so he too, had to be destroyed.

Some time afterward, a fourth and last attempt was made. Four animals are said to have shown the gods where to obtain the necessary material—a ground corn—to make an intelligent being who would remember his Creators.

The Four Animals led the way to two villages, Paxil and Cayala.

According to the Popul-Vuh, Zmucane, the Grandmother, prepared the materials for the flesh of mankind. She ground together the white and yellow maize and made "nine drinks." Then Tepeu and Gucumatz took the cornmeal dough she made for them and made four men, the first "fathers of the human race." These were wise men, versed in magic, without ancestors, and they were the first representatives of humanity as it now exists on earth.

This somewhat amusing account from the Popul-Vuh is

obviously a lot of mythology, fairy lore, and legend, but, nevertheless, does tie in to a great extent with the manufacture of humanity as given in Genesis.

There are many other similar accounts of the manufacture of humanity in the folklore of other countries.

However, it would seem that since the Sky People made and put us here, they have not only continued to pay visits to our planet, but to interbreed with us. For what purpose?

25

Are We a Hybrid Race?

Darwin's theory of evolution is widely accepted as regards life in general, but in the case of mankind it has one drawback. The emergence of the brain of mankind on this planet was too quick. Even Darwin was worried on this score and realized that natural selection might not be the complete answer in respect of mankind. It has long been appreciated that there is a hypothetical "missing link."

A contemporary American writer, Otto O. Binder, states emphatically "that mankind appeared so suddenly on the scene because he was a planned hybrid, a cross between superintelligent sky people and subintelligent ape-men on Earth."[73]

Binder quoted from a revolutionary book called *On Tiptoe Beyond Darwin,* by Max H. Flindt. The author posed the question, Is it because man's brain is an import?

Flindt wrote: "Except for man, the best that nature could do on land was to develop three great ape families. This means that it took nature 500 million years to develop one million neurons (the maximum capacity of an anthropoid brain). At this rate, one neuron was developed every six months . . . [and] man, with his ten billion neurons, should have taken ten times as long as the apes in order to develop his fantastic brain.

"Ten times 500 million years is five billion years."

Binder comments: "Yet man and his superb thinking organ, they would have us believe, came out of the evolutionary pot in a mere two million years.

"Obviously, nature did not create man's brain. The sky-men did in an ancient breeding experiment or a series of them."

Is there any evidence for this startling theory? I suggest that there is a case to be examined. I have already given some indication in the last two chapters that the Sky People put us here. However, there are legends all over the world indicating that the gods came down to earth and mingled with us mortals. The Mayans, Aztecs, Incas, Etruscans, ancient Egyptians, Greeks, North American Indians, Hawaiians, Scandinavians, Chinese, Japanese, Indians, and Irish all relate similar accounts of godlike beings visiting them in ancient times.

Admittedly, all this stems from mythology, legend, and folklore, but when so many diverse peoples scattered all over the world recount similar tales, it surely must be significant.

Then there are the famous verses in Genesis which definitely report mating between extraterrestrials and terrestrials: "That the sons of God saw the daughters of men that they were fair; and they took them wives of all which they chose." (Genesis 6:2) "There were giants in the earth in those days; and also after that, when the sons of God came in unto the daughters of men, and they bare children to them, the same became mighty men which were of old, men of renown." (Genesis 6:4)

One of the first known civilizations of which we have records is that of Sumeria. Dr. Carl Sagan, of Harvard University and the Smithsonian Astrophysical Observatory, co-authored with Dr. I. S. Shklovskii, of the Sternberg Astronomical Institute, Soviet Academy of Sciences, a notable work entitled *Intelligent Life in the Universe.*[74]

In the book, Dr. Sagan commented on the fact that such a brilliant civilization should have suddenly emerged from nowhere. He came across a legend of special quality and stated that it was of great interest as it related to the origin of the Sumerian civilization. No one knows where the Sumerians originated. Sagan feels that if the Sumerian civilization was described by their descendants to be of extraterrestrial origin, then legends such as this one (the Apkallu) should be examined thoroughly. He was careful to add that the legend described in his book was not necessarily an example of contact between humans and nonhumans, but it was of a caliber that deserved more careful study. The legend tells of contact being made on the shores of the Persian Gulf in the fourth millennium B.C., or earlier. Dr. Sagan goes on to say that the earth may have been visited by galactic civilizations many times in antiquity. We have mentioned this interesting legend, if only to point out that some of the new breed of enlightened scientists today are prepared to consider that we have been visited in the past by Sky People.

Now, in our earlier chapters in this section, we postulated that the first creation given in Genesis was that of Galactic Man. It is our idea that Galactic Man may be the inhabitant of billions of planets in our chemical universe.

Scientists today concede that there are millions of planets in our galaxy alone which may be inhabited by intelligent thinking beings. Is it not possible that there may be a superfederation of galactic planets?

Fred Hoyle, Plumian Professor of Astronomy at Cambridge University, in his book *Of Men and Galaxies*, wrote: "You are all familiar with an ordinary telephone directory. You want to speak to someone, you look up his number, and you dial the appropriate code. My speculation is that a similar situation exists, and has existed for billions of years, in the Galaxy. My speculation is that an interchange of messages is going on, on a vast scale, all the time, and that we are as unaware of it as a pygmy in the African forests is unaware of the radio messages that flash at the speed of light around the earth. My guess is there might be a million or more subscribers to the galactic directory. Our problem is to get our name into that directory."[75]

There may well be a central galactic civilization which has

steadily colonized all the habitable planets, including earth, over a long period of time. They may have conducted a series of breeding experiments at different stages of our long history, and may now be watching our development with great interest.

However, we can be certain of one thing. If the Sky People have periodically mated with earth people to hasten mankind's evolution, the brain capacity of sky people must be far superior to that of earth men. Flindt, mentioned earlier, postulates that the Sky People must have a brain capacity of at least 3000 cubic centimeters compared with a human's 1300 cubic centimeters today. A breeding program between Sky People and earlier ape men with about 800 cubic centimeters' capacity would have produced the middle brain of modern man. If so, the biblical comment that we were made higher than the animals and lower than the angels is only too true.

Possibly, the Sky People are still breeding with us. We might not learn of such a happening. Who would dare state that he or she had had a sexual experience with an extraterrestrial? And, if they did so, who would believe them? However, this has happened in modern times, if we believe the account of Antonio Villas-Boas, a young Brazilian farmer. His story has been given in full detail over many issues of *Flying Saucer Review,* and also related in several books. His account has been very fully investigated by the late Dr. Olavo Fontes, who undoubtedly considered it a true experience.[76]

How do we know for certain that other similar cases have not occurred? Antonio Villas-Boas was extremely reluctant to relate his experiences and this is most understandable. If it is true that interbreeding between the two races of mankind and elsewhere is still going on today, then the brain capacity of mankind in the future may be advanced from 1300 cubic centimeters to somewhere nearer that of the Sky People. Indeed, *this could be the long-range plan.*

The ideas expressed here are highly controversial, but the concept of Sky People interbreeding with humanity does explain the "missing link." There is no other factor that can account for the far too rapid evolution of mankind's brain, which is contrary to Darwin's theory of natural selection and the normal gradual evolution of a species by nature. Perhaps, after all, we are a hybrid race, partly descended from superintelligent Sky People and subintelligent ape men.

Why is it that mankind alone, apart from all other species on this planet, when he is not fighting wars or enmeshed with his daily worries, has a sense of destiny? Deep down inside, mankind subconsciously knows that he is part of some tremendous cosmic scheme. If we are, indeed, a hybrid race, then one day we may take our place in a much wider civilization —a galactic one. This would be in every sense "a giant leap for mankind."

This Cosmic Concept, if you can accept it, does explain why the occupants of the UFOs today have such a great interest in us. It would seem that they have made and put us here in the first place, and subsequently interbred with us. They have watched our progress over thousands of years, involving catastrophes upon our planet, and are still with us today while we take our first brave steps into space.

26

History Repeats Itself

On November 13, 1970, the London *Evening Standard* (followed by the next day's morning papers, TV, and radio) broke the news that a British scientist, Dr. James Danielli, and his two assistants from King's College in London, had produced the simplest form of life, by putting in a test tube pieces of living cells. They knew success had been achieved when they looked down their microscopes at New York State University in Buffalo and saw that the cells had broken apart on their own, and had reproduced themselves hundreds of times.

Dr. Danielli predicted that new animals, new plants, and new microorganisms would eventually be synthesized using this method. He considered that a human living creature could be made eventually—possibly in twenty years!

This scientist is fully aware of the unscrupulous use power-hungry men may make of his breakthrough in this field. For example, by juggling the genes and chromosomes, you could make a docile race or a brutal one of fighting men. A frightening thought.

However, it now seems that humanity is going to take its turn at usurping the role of the Elohim. We are going to imitate them and make a race of humans who, no doubt, will be required *to serve, guard and keep our garden.*

Strange, how history repeats itself!

PART FIVE

The Tremendous Tomorrow

27

The New Race

Jacques Bergier and Louis Pauwels in the concluding chapter of their book *Morning of the Magicians* engage in a fascinating discussion as to whether a race of mutants is being born among us today. One reason given was that the amount of strontium 90 in the atmosphere as the result of nuclear experiments has affected the human genes, and caused new children to be born with a much higher I.Q. This is certainly an intriguing idea.

It is, certainly, noticeable that young people today, generally speaking, are very different from previous generations. There is much talk about the "generation gap," the differences and lack of understanding between many parents and their children.

There have, of course, always been some differences and disagreements between parents and children throughout the ages, but never to such an extent as today. Furthermore, these differences are not confined to those between parents and children, but reach out to those between the younger generation and the establishment in every department that you can visualize.

The new race of young people have brought about radical changes in many spheres. For example, in music, painting, sculpture, the theater, dress and hair styles, and in attitudes toward life generally.

The music and lyrics of the Beatles, the Rolling Stones,

and other groups, were absolutely different from anything that had been heard before. It caught on like wildfire with young people everywhere, who instinctively identified themselves with the sounds. As I write these words I am listening to a song being broadcast by BBC Radio Four on their *Late Night Extra* program called "We're Going to Change the World." That is the mood of the younger generation today.

A complete revolution has been achieved. Young men and women, both with long hair and colorful attire—it is often difficult to determine which of a pair is the male or female—walk our streets today like visitors from some far-off planet.

They have made themselves a force to be reckoned with on university campuses throughout the world. Even that great man de Gaulle had difficulty in coping with the student revolts in the streets of Paris.

Another point well worth bearing in mind is that an enormous number of the young today are interested in magic, witchcraft, psychic phenomena, and extrasensory perception. They are searching for a deeper awareness of themselves and of the cosmos. I sometimes get the impression they are trying to find something that is their heritage—something with which they are really familiar. Some of them use drugs. That is to be deplored, but that scene is all part of the picture.

Their morals, their outlook on life generally, are completely different from that of their elders. They speak a different language.

Now, the startling idea I am trying to put over is that this new race of young people could be an alien one! Of course, I am not saying that they are extraterrestrials, but that due to the effects of strontium 90 it is possible that some additional characteristics or influences have got into their basic make-up.

Bergier and Pauwels wrote: "Two American scientists, C. Brooke Worth and Robert K. Enders, in an important work entitled *The Nature of Living Things,* believe there is proof that the genes groups have been disturbed and that, under the influence of forces that are still mysterious, a new race of men is appearing, endowed with superior intellectual powers. This is, of course, a subject to be approached with caution. The genetician Lewis Terman, however, after thirty years study of infant prodigies, has reached the following conclusions: Most infant prodigies used in the past to lose their faculties on becoming adult. It would seem today that they tend to become a superior kind of adult, *gifted with an intelligence that has nothing in common with that of ordinary human beings.* They are thirty times as active as a normal man of talent. Their 'success index' is multiplied by twenty-five. Their health is perfect, as well as their sentimental and sexual balance. Finally, they escape the psychosomatic diseases, notably cancer. Is this certain? One thing is certain, and that is that we are now witnessing a progressive acceleration throughout the world of the mental faculties, and this is also true of the physical. The phenomenon is so evident that another American scientist, Dr. Sydney Pressey, of the University of Ohio, has just drawn up a plan for the instruction of precocious children capable, in his opinion, of producing 300,000 superior intelligences a year." (Italics mine).

It would seem that we are now experiencing a period of infiltration of our species, perhaps comparable to the advent of Cro-Magnon man thousands of years ago. Incidentally, Ape man had been on this planet for some thousands of years before the arrival of Cro-Magnon man. It is possible, and I throw this idea out for what it is worth, that Cro-Magnon man who arrived very suddenly and a definite advance on his predecessors, was the new Hu-man made by the Elohim. Cro-Magnon man is said by various experts, who always disagree, to have arrived here very suddenly, sometime between fifty and a hundred thousand years ago.

My remarks that the last two decades are bringing forth a new race of children should not upset the parents. The children do, of course, take on the hereditary characteristics of their fathers and mothers, and look like them physically, but are blessed, generally speaking, with higher intelligence and are physically better endowed than previous generations.

We must not be frightened of change. For far too long we have stagnated in a rut. The new race of young people have succeeded in jolting us out of it to some extent. Not all change is necessarily a good thing, but let's face it, very often we don't like it because the old way of life had become so familiar. If we are going to live in the new space age it is essential to be able to cope with change. To illustrate this better, I am going to quote from a delightful science-fiction book called *Out of This World,* by Ben Barzman.[77]

"What was it about him? Then it hit me. Wilfred was perfectly at home. It didn't matter that it was another planet and that he had flown through space and that we were participating in a fabulous event. Wilfred felt at ease. He belonged. He was a part of it.

"He had always been a part of it. That had always been his quality whether it was a geisha house in Nagasaki or a London drawing room, or arguing with my uncle Debret.

"I think I figured out why. *It was because he accepted nothing as permanently fixed, people, institutions, values.* There wasn't a goddam thing you couldn't change—if you felt they needed changing.

"When you feel that way you're no longer scared. You're at ease. You can do something about it, handle it.

"Not like me. If you don't walk into a snug ready-made world with hot and cold running comfort you've had it, I hear myself say to myself. You can only cross your fingers and hope for the best.

"That's why anything new scares you. Wilfred finally bought it in a plane anyway but while he lived he was alive. He didn't let two-thirds of himself go down the drain in vague fears and apologizing for being alive. . . . I suddenly felt exhilarated. I had made a discovery as important, it seemed to me, as discovering a twin planet. I'd found out why I'd been afraid." (Italics mine.)

Our young people today are not afraid of change. They

welcome it. Like Wilfred in the extract from the science-fiction story just related, they are at ease with the new way of life.

We have been spelling out in no uncertain terms the possibility that our planet is in the process of being taken over by a new race—quite unconsciously, of course—which is being born here as a result of strontium 90 affecting the human genes. These new children, many of them now adult, may not be aware of the possibility that mysterious forces have endowed them with superior intellectual powers. A few may question their marked abilities and ponder over them. I wouldn't know. In any case, I am not criticizing the younger generation, but merely pointing out that, generally speaking, they are completely different from previous generations.

There is, of course, a minority of teenagers that spend their spare time spoiling other people's pleasure, wantonly damaging property at holiday resorts and, generally, making a nuisance of themselves. These young people are in a different category. Their moronic behavior is due, in part, to overcrowding and lack of local facilities to release their pent-up energies. They, too, want to bring about change, but in their misguided way vent their angry frustrations on their fellow beings. However, although they make the front pages of our newspapers they are a minority and not really typical of the younger generation.

Despite these militant teenage gangs and the drug addicts, it is our contention that, taken by and large, the new generation is a remarkable phenomenon.

John A. Keel, the American ufologist, has hinted that our planet is in the process of being taken over by what he calls "ultra-terrestrials." This is an interesting name. He implies that they are already here. However, as far as I know he did not state that they were the new race of young people. On the other hand, he also implied that many people today on this planet were being "manipulated" or influenced. Well, according to Bergier and Pauwels, the younger generation born among us has been influenced by mysterious forces from out-side. In any case, it seems to me a very progressive and good influence.

Along with the new race now born among us, we have the manifestations of flying-saucer and psychic activity that have been intensifying *during the same two decades.* This is no mere coincidence!

It could be—and this is pure speculation—that the new children are the "advance guard" for the coming of the Sky People. As we have already pointed out, they are extremely receptive to and interested in what are termed New Age sub-jects.

Another point to be borne in mind is that these young people will be the rulers of the world in a few years time. They will fill the positions of responsibility in politics, industry, communications, astronautics, and the arts. Some do so al-ready.

Many people think that we are approaching the end of a cycle or an age, and that we are in what they call the "latter days." Perhaps we are. In short, that we are on the threshold of big events, such as an Armageddon or some natural catas-trophe involving a "flip" of the poles. They point to the prob-lems of overpopulation, pollution, and possible worldwide famine, as well as to the increasing number of wars and earth-quakes. They cite the general increase of crime and skuldug-gery. Other pointers are the general all-around degeneration of morals and the emphasis on sex, and finally, biblical prophecies about the end of this age.

Nevertheless, though some of these doomsday prophecies may come to pass, I take an optimistic view. I have faith in this new young generation. Although we hear a lot about hippies and "layabouts," there are now some very talented and gifted young people of both sexes among us. I think that if the genes have been disturbed through the effects of stron-tium 90, we have been given another of those "shots in the arm" referred to earlier, and that our young people will lead us to the stars. Maybe, to another Golden Age.

28

The Lattice

All through history there have been groups of people who were the possessors of certain knowledge that has been handed down from generation to generation. It was passed on to new, carefully selected and initiated keepers by Masons, mystery schools and other esoteric groups, who in turn worked with it and kept the secrets. This knowledge was the Secret Wisdom, and today it is becoming more widely known than hitherto, because we are living in the age of Aquarius.

The true mysteries are still kept secret by those who respect their trust, and there are many real occultists who do not exploit their knowledge. On the other hand, the scientific world is rapidly learning the secrets of the esotericist. Bergier and Pauwels have pointed out that our advanced modern physicists are the alchemists of today. Unfortunately, what the physicist learns today, the politician will use tomorrow for military and aggressive ends, certainly not desired by the originators of the Mysteries. That is one of the reasons such care was used to keep secret or hidden (the word *occult* means hidden) the Secret Wisdom.

The secrecy imposed by the mystery schools has nothing in common with the suppressions of certain truths by the church a few centuries after the birth of Christianity. This was something different—a desire for control and power. At one time the church had much more temporal power than it has now. The real Initiate or Man of Wisdom does not wish to control his fellows.

That is why the Master Alchemist Fulcanelli, after completing his literary masterpiece, *Le Mystère des Cathédrales,* handed it over to Eugène Cansiliet, who was studying under him, and disappeared immediately afterward. This was in 1928, when Fulcanelli was seventy-two. Legend has it that the alchemist is still alive in the flesh, that he had made the last adeptus transformation, and now, like the equally legendary St.-Germain, is living in the world under another name with the appearance of a man in his forties.[78]

We suggest that his disappearance was due to the fact that his knowledge was beyond price and would be too invaluable to be given out to a materialistic world that would abuse it. It is said that the intelligence services of several countries have vainly tried to trace him.

Undoubtedly, there have been people in the past centuries who were familiar with the Ancient Wisdom, men who worked together and communicated with each other. It was something more than a network of Minds. The term *lattice* in the sense of a crystal structure illustrates the concept better.

I would like to suggest that in the Fourfold Cosmos there is a "lattice," too, that each member of it works, functions, behaves, lives, moves, and has his being as if *alone.* Yet, under proper conditions each is accessible to all. Each has his store of data. Like a tiny component in a great modern computer, each is *itself*—yet, without it, no answer given out by the complete lattice would be entirely correct.

It is my contention that people on this earth have been able to contact this lattice, and that is where they have gotten their inspirations and discoveries.

Once again, it is appreciated that this is a highly controversial suggestion.

How does one hook into this lattice?

I would suggest that all Men (Elohim) are hooked into it irrevocably since the first day of Creation.

Nevertheless, humans can, I suggest, contact the Lattice, by the time-honored methods of "sleeping with the idea," prayer, and meditation.

It may well be argued that surely it is sufficient to direct your supplications directly to God Himself. The point is well taken. However, He is no doubt very busy and He has, in my humble opinion, a Lattice. So why not use it and send your questions to His able lieutenants waiting to give the answers? Rather like going up the normal channels in the civil service, only in this case the service is more efficient.

Now, you may ask what has this all got to do with the UFOs. Well, it has quite a lot. Actually, the UFOs are only a side effect of a very big operation. To us ufologists they are very important, or seem to be. However, when you look into this subject in depth, they are only vehicles bringing the ufonauts here.

The real interest is why are they coming here? It is my idea that we have been made and put here, that the Makers are concerned with developing us unobtrusively—in short, that we make the grade ourselves—with occasional "shots in the arm," and eventually, that we will take our place in the galactic civilization.

One way in which we can make progress is through contact with the lattice. I appreciate that this is a hypothetical idea, but many occultists down the centuries will vouch for its existence. Anyway, it is more celestial food for thought.

29

The Instantaneous
Way to the Stars

In *Operation Earth* I used the title "The Way to the Stars" as a chapter heading, and I think that it should be included again here with the addition of one all-important word. Since the original chapter was written, some very exciting ideas have been aired.

However, first let us digress for a moment. Some years ago, a very distinguished British astronomer was interviewed on a TV program about UFOs. He stated that they could not possibly come from our solar system because our probes had established that no life could exist there (he may be right on this point, but it remains to be completely proven), and that they could not come here from elsewhere in the galaxy because of the tremendous distance involved, and anyway, nothing could possibly exceed the speed of light.

No doubt at the time this distinguished man gave this interview that may have been the accepted scientific view, though I rather think that even then some of our more enlightened scientists were looking to the possibilities of stellar travel, quite apart from how UFOs could come here.

Today, our new breed of scientists do not look at far-reaching concepts and condemn them out of hand because they are not in accordance with accepted scientific thought. They think, "This is an interesting idea. We will not necessarily accept nor discard it. We will examine it thoroughly and see if anything else comes along to give it some validity." In fact, today many of our most respected scientists are coming up themselves with really fantastic ideas, as we shall see.

In *Operation Earth* I wrote: "Some scientists (there are some forward-thinking ones) realize that it is possible to travel faster than the speed of light. When this happens we get beyond the limits of space and time into an unknown area, 'the Eternal Now,' that the mystics talk about.

"You see, as we pass the speed of light, 'time,' as it is known to us, ceases to exist. And then strange things happen. For the simple reason that human 'time' has stopped, our thinking changes. We are now in a different continuum, a new universe."

For many years now, science-fiction writers have been telling us about a hypothetical area called hyperspace into which their imaginary space ships entered—where, as I wrote in *Operation Earth*, "we get beyond the limits of space and time, into an unknown area"—and, by using this unknown route, the distance and time to the stars is shortened to an incredible degree. In fact, as we shall see later, travel to the stars becomes instantaneous!

Recently, the London *Daily Telegraph* color magazine ran a series of three fascinating science articles by Adrian Berry.[79] The second one discussed Professor John A. Wheeler's interpretation of Albert Einstein's general theory of relativity, completed around 1916, following upon the special theory of relativity, which appeared in 1905. Professor Wheeler's study and interpretation of Einstein's general theory brings the whole idea of hyperspace within the realm of probability. Dr. Wheeler is professor of physics at Princeton University.

In a paper delivered in 1962, the professor visualized that space contains, as he termed them, "wormholes," or entrances into another universe, which he called "superspace," akin to the "hyperspace" of science-fiction writers.

Einstein pointed out that there is no such thing as a straight line. Space is curved, believe it or not. However, this curvature is only noticeable over a very wide area. The reason everything is curved in space is an effect of gravitational forces.

The *Daily Telegraph* color magazine showed a picture of Professor Wheeler holding a doughnut with its traditional hole in the middle. They also depicted a "doughnut" model of the universe. To quote: "All the stars and galaxies are on the curved solid surface of the doughnut. The hole inside represents the mysterious region of Superspace, in which space and time do not exist. All journeys through it are therefore instantaneous. A signal—or spaceship—traveling directly across Superspace might be able to reach its destination in no time at all, in contrast to a journey round the curved surface which would take centuries. . . ."

Apparently, space is not just nothing but actually a solid! It has holes in it just like a piece of smooth furniture seen under a powerful microscope.

Professor Wheeler's work and tentative conclusions are especially interesting to me, because they seem to be validating my Cosmic Concept, which was first published in a much deeper form in 1964. As you will recall, I postulated that our chemical universe, and that includes its space, is inside what I termed the Cosmic Emotional Universe (one of the Fourfold Cosmic Universes).

Now, you see that Professor Wheeler suggests that Superspace—an area where time and space, as we know it, does not exist—is basically there and that the solidified "doughnut" of galaxies, suns, planets, and our space, exists in it. You can well imagine how thrilled I was to read about Professor Wheeler's work!

We are still a long way off from putting Professor Wheeler's theory to practical purposes. For instance, where are the "wormholes"?

An immediate question comes to my inquisitive mind. It is this. Do Ivan Sanderson's ten "vile vortices" discussed in Chapter Fourteen have any connection with the professor's "wormholes"? Could they be major entrances on this planet to "hyperspace" or "Superspace"?

Everything in this universe seems to be arranged in a very mathematical way. Therefore, it seems to me that Sanderson's ten vortices, which are also placed in an orderly, geometrical manner, may prove to be the key to this enigma.

Be that as it may, what is now becoming more and more apparent is that someday—it may be a long way off yet—we will be able to reach the stars through what the science-fiction writers call hyperspace, and Professor Wheeler terms Superspace.

It is absolutely amazing how science-fiction writers, over and over again, seem to have the knack of hitting the nail on the head, by predicting in advance the realities of tomorrow. I sometimes think that their minds are influenced and inspired, probably unknown to themselves, by our mysterious visitors. They would probably deny this suggestion. These splendid, imaginative, and creative writers would no doubt state that the ideas were their own. That in a sense is true. But, I question whether any real idea is entirely our own. However, right now I would like to pay tribute to the wonderful line of science-fiction writers who have done so much to entertain us, stir our imaginations, and predict so accurately many of the wonders that have come to pass. We salute H. G. Wells, Jules Verne, and also Jonathan Swift. I include the last for his accurate assessment of the two satellites of Mars—Phobus and Deimos—in *Gulliver's Travels,* 150 years before they were officially discovered by Asaph Hall, the American astronomer, in 1877.[80]

In our own time, we have such giants as Isaac Asimov, Arthur C. Clarke, Robert A. Heinlein, John W. Campbell, Theodore Sturgeon, Poul Anderson, Clifford Simak, and many others of this brilliant fraternity.

In particular, Asimov has done a tremendous job in propagating the idea of a galactic civilization in his stories and also of writing about hyperspace.

So it seems that one day we will travel to the stars through Asimov's hyperspace, but surely, the corollary could also take effect.

If we can go to the stars in this manner, then the Sky People can come here, despite what the respected British astronomer said some years ago.

Another point. If the UFOs suddenly manifest out of "wormholes" or "vile vortices" on the earth's surface, it is possible they would escape the radar network that our politicians are always telling us the UFOs can't get through without being detected.

It has always seemed to me a bit naïve when Ministers in the House of Commons have stated in answer to a question about UFO activity that the UFOs couldn't get through our radar network without being spotted.

These official statements always seem to show a lack of vision and are just giving an appreciation of the situation based on our present knowledge, as if it were the Russians or the Chinese trying to get their aircraft unseen through our radar network.

Does it not strike any of these eminent gentlemen that an alien race which has had space travel for millennia would by now have discovered a means of entering our air space without being detected by our silly old radar of which we are so rightly proud?

They probably have systems far more advanced and ways of evading our radar brought to a very high state of excellence. I have long ago reached the stage of reading statements by Ministers on this subject in the national press with a pinch of salt.

The fact is, the flying saucers can come and go as they like, and our aircraft and radar can do nothing about it. There are many reports on record that prove this. They have been seen on radar and visually from the ground. They have also been seen visually in the air and from the ground, but *not* picked up by radar in the vicinity. So they can pick and choose what they want to do.

We are really in their hands. There is nothing we can do about it. However, for reasons expressed earlier, I do not think the real Sky People are hostile to us. It is my contention that they put us here and are watching over our development. There do seem to be some hostile ones pertaining to the invisible area around our planet, and that is the accepted view of many leading ufologists. However, the real Sky People who live "far out," it would seem, are keeping a weather eye on us. In a sense, as Charles Fort stated in one of his remarkable books, "We are property."[81]

Yes, it could be said that we are property, for as you have seen—if you go along with the traditional stories from all over the world—we were made by them, put here, and since then they have interbred with us, watched our development, and injected "shots in the arm." So, all right, it could be said they own us, but I do not think they regard us in that light any more. When humans were first made they were an unknown quantity. Now, with some slight assistance, we have come a long way and are graduating for membership in a galactic civilization. In time, we will be possibly "kicked upstairs" into the Cosmic Emotional Universe as fully fledged members—at least some of us will, after the planet has settled its present chaotic period of transition, change and general upheaval—spiritually, mentally, physically, and economically.

The *Daily Telegraph* color magazine ended its second science article by stating about Wheeler, "This extraordinary thinker, who has developed the theories of Einstein just as Einstein himself modified and enlarged upon the laws of Sir Isaac Newton, is doing work today that may one day give us a Galactic Empire."

I would like to rewrite the end of this concluding paragraph in the article as follows: "is doing work today that may one day give us the opportunity of being accepted in a Galactic Civilization."

It is always the human idea to conquer and take over. There may be other intelligences in the galaxy waiting and hoping for us to join them, but not on take-over terms. We will have to learn to live the galactic way and a little less, the violent human one.

30

Time Is Short

We started this book by giving a review of the worldwide UFO situation and mentioned the mysterious part of intelligence agencies in attempting to play down the whole business. It was postulated that the authorities appreciated that the UFOs were paranormal, and that probably they did not have all the answers. If they were to announce that UFOs were real, then they would have some very awkward questions to answer. Better play it cool and hope that the maddening UFOs would go away.

Despite the Condon Commission's negative conclusions being given wide newspaper coverage and their publication in paperback form, there is a tremendous interest in the subject. We have only to witness the enormous worldwide success of Erich von Daniken's books dealing with the possibility that Sky People may have visited us in ancient times to realize this.[82]

It is possible that as more people become aware of the reality of the UFOs (there are now hundreds of UFO groups throughout the world) then a general acceptance could come from the public themselves.

From time to time, articles appear in the press and magazines highlighting new scientific discoveries. The *Daily Telegraph* color magazine's series of scientific articles, discussed in the last chapter, has done a signal service in writing about Professor Wheeler's concept of Superspace and suggesting that one day we may be able to reach the stars in no time at all. Those readers of the article who have been told that UFOs cannot come here because of the vast distances involved will possibly think again.

Gradually, as this theme of Wheeler's develops—and, you can be sure we will hear more of it—the idea will be implanted without anyone's saying so, that the UFOs could come here, after all. Then, as I say, a gradual, general acceptance of their reality may come from the public themselves, without an official announcement. A *fait accompli*. All this, of course, would delight the authorities, and help them over a difficult hurdle.

However, it would seem imperative to bring about this general recognition in the shortest possible time, and furthermore to develop the practical side of Professor Wheeler's theory as soon as possible.

We know about the growing dangers of pollution to our food, our air, our oceans, and our land, as well as to the animals, birds, fish, and ourselves. We have also been told about the overpopulation problem and the worldwide famine which may grow to astronomical proportions, engulfing the west, as well as the east.

Additionally, we know that there are more wars going on all over the world than at any previous time in history. The Middle East situation is still not resolved and could explode into a Third World War at any moment.

It is more than obvious that our civilization cannot go on like this for very much longer. It would seem that the crunch is coming. Whether it will take the form of a series of worldwide catastrophes, as foretold by the Seer of Virginia Beach, the late Edgar Cayce, who had an incredible number of "bull's-eyes" to his credit,[83] or an Armageddon, or perhaps both, it is impossible to predict. Quite seriously, it would seem that something will have to act as a catalyst. I know that in an earlier chapter I took an optimistic view, but I did state that some of these events might come to pass.

On the other hand, patterns can change. A seer can predict

something quite genuinely based on what is seen ahead in his own time. However, circumstances can alter, and these changes could throw the seer's predictions.

It seems to me that Professor Wheeler's theory about Superspace could bring about a correction in the predicted pattern, provided that the work is expedited.

The greatest problem at the moment is overpopulation. Most of the other worldwide problems derive from that one —famine, housing, pollution, and even wars. World population in the next few decades is going to snowball to an alarming degree.

If Professor Wheeler's ideas can be developed and turned to practical use within the next few years, then we will be able to reach other star systems, and perhaps, find uninhabited planets. Then, large portions of our population will be able to emigrate to these new worlds, as our ancestors sailed overseas to the new land of America.

Incidentally, too, Adrian Berry, in his first article in the *Daily Telegraph* color magazine, had an amazing proposition which links up with what I have just suggested.

He mentioned the imaginative ideas of Professor Carl Sagan, whom we quoted earlier in this book. He has a scheme to change the environment of Venus so that our people could live there. As we all know, our satellite probes of Venus have indicated that it has an unbearably hot temperature on the surface of 800° Fahrenheit.

Incidentally, at one time Venus was thought to have a much lower temperature. When Dr. Immanuel Velikovsky, in his book *Worlds in Collision,* stated the opposite, this was one of the many points that the scientists at the time of publication of his book came down heavily on him about, and indeed, there was a big furor. I am happy that not only on this point of the temperature of Venus, but on others, Dr. Velikovsky has been completely vindicated.[84]

Sagan's fantastic idea is to send a few hundred algae-bearing rockets to Venus to produce rain and turn that planet into a habitable place for us.

Well, as you can see, some of the greatest minds in the world are turning their attention to resolving ways in which humanity may be able to move out from this overcrowded planet earth into the galaxy and live on renovated worlds. And that they will reach them through Superspace.

All these concepts are beyond the average thinking of most people. The advanced scientist of today is way out ahead. Modern technology and thinking is moving now at a stupendous pace. They may yet beat the catastrophe barrier discussed at the beginning of this chapter. And you can be sure that "the boys upstairs" will be behind them!

We have been based on Mother Earth long enough. It is time some of our more adventurous young people went off exploring the Cosmos, the way, in the last Elizabethan Age, our seamen found new lands in the Americas. In this present Elizabethan Age our astronauts, using Professor Wheeler's Superspace route to the stars, may find new worlds to populate in the galaxy. This is a magnificent task, not beyond human capabilities. So, you see, there is a Tremendous Tomorrow.

It is our destiny to take our place in the galactic civilization which some of us believe to exist.

Undoubtedly, the greatest story in the world today is that of the Sky People. The flying saucers are still with us. They have always been around, keeping watch over us. They started it all eons ago, the long saga of the flying-saucer story. The fascinating celestial chariots of yesterday, the UFOs of today.

Appendix A.
Descriptions of UFO Shapes

The general public is not aware of the infinite variety of UFO shapes and sizes that have been reported. Therefore, the following descriptions of UFO types will come as an eye-opener to some of our readers.

This information has been supplied by the Data Research Division of Contact (U.K.) and is taken from their publication *The UFO Register,* vol. 1, part 2, 1970.

The UFOs have been divided into common or comparatively common types and less common (or rare) types.

COMMON OR RELATIVELY COMMON TYPES

Code	*Description of Type*
1a	FLAT DISC: round, domeless.
1b	FLAT DISC: multi-sided, domeless.
1c	FLAT DISC: round, centrally domed. Domes variable in size.
1d	DUSTBIN LID-SHAPED: round, sub-pyramidal, mostly domeless.
2	HAT-SHAPED: central cabin vertically cylindrical (but often rounded on top) encircled ventrally by a flat rim.
3a	BOWL- OR DISH-SHAPED: round, domeless.

3b	BOWL- OR DISH-SHAPED: round, domed.
4	SAUCER-SHAPED: round, centrally domed. Domes variously shaped.
5a	DOUBLE SAUCER: lightly convex round units joined peripherally.
5b	DOUBLE SAUCER: marked by convex round units similarly joined.
6	RUGBY BALL-SHAPED: domeless.
6a	RUGBY BALL-SHAPED: centrally domed. Dome usually very small.
7	SATURN-SHAPED.
8a	SPHERE OR GLOBE: plain-surfaced.
8b	SPHERE OR GLOBE: surface paneled or segmented.
8c	SPHERE OR GLOBE: tailed. Tails of various shapes and sizes.
8d	SPHERE OR GLOBE: domed. Dome usually small.
9	EGG-SHAPED.
10	"ROUND": either type 8a (or indistinguishable variants) or types 1a or 1c to 4 viewed full face.
11	"OVAL" or "ELLIPTICAL": either that shape, or types 1 to 5a viewed obliquely.
12	"PYRAMIDAL": pitch to apex variable (probably a variant of 1d).
13a	CONE-SHAPED (often described as bulletlike): one end rounded.
13b	CONE-SHAPED: one end pointed.
14a	ROCKET-SHAPED: single- or multifinned.
14b	ROCKET-SHAPED: finless.
15	ARROW-SHAPED: length variable.
16	TORPEDO-SHAPED (including "sausage"-shaped forms).
17a	CIGAR-SHAPED.
17b	CIGAR-SHAPED: dorsally domed.
17c	CIGAR-SHAPED: domed dorsally and ventrally.
18a	CYLINDER-SHAPED: diameter uniform throughout.
18b	CYLINDER-SHAPED: wholly or partially tapered.
18c	FUNNEL- OR BELL-SHAPED.

19   RODLIKE: usually very thin (possibly a variant of 18a).

20   BAR-SHAPED: lengths and thickness highly variable.

21   BARREL-SHAPED.

22   BULBLIKE OR PEAR-SHAPED.

23   HUMMING OR SPINNING TOP-SHAPED.

24   MUSHROOM-SHAPED.

25   DOUGHNUT-SHAPED: central "hole" of variable diameter.

26a   RING-SHAPED: single.

26b   RING-SHAPED: double or multiple.

26c   COIL-OR SPRING-SHAPED.

27a   WHEEL-SHAPED: spoked.

27b   WHEEL-SHAPED: cogged. Objects described as jagged-edged discs are included in this category.

28   SPINDLE-SHAPED.

29   CROSS-SHAPED: possibly a variant of type 14a.

30   MULTIARMED: generally a small central globe having three or more radiating arms, often independantly movable.

31   TENTACLED: generally a small central globe with trailing or hanging flexible "arms."

32a   CRESCENT-SHAPED.

32b   V-SHAPED OR BOOMERANG-SHAPED: coordinated lights moving in a V-like formation seem frequently to be the illuminated portions of an otherwise blacked-out V-shaped UFO.

32c   D-SHAPED OR HEELLIKE.

32d   DELTAWING-SHAPED: occasionally with a short fuselage.

41a   FLAT TRIANGLE: domeless.

41b   FLAT TRIANGLE: domed. Dome usually very small. Position variable.

42   DIAMOND- OR LOZENGE-SHAPED: nearly always domeless.

43   OBLONG-SHAPED: usually four-dimensional.

44a   SQUARE- OR RECTANGLE-SHAPED: flat.

44b SQUARE OR RECTANGLE-SHAPED: four dimensional.
45 DIFFUSE OR CLOUDLIKE: probably directly connected
with one or more solid objects hidden within. Cases
are known where solid objects entered or emerged
from erratically but independantly moving cloudlike
masses.
46 GLOBULAR LIGHTS: probably solid objects obscured by
luminosity.
47 STARLIKE: probably solid objects obscured by luminosity.
48 FLARELIKE.
49 TADPOLE-SHAPED.
50 SQUIGGLY-SHAPED: highly flexible objects, often alter-
ing shape continuously.

UNCOMMON AND RARE TYPES

51 RAILWAY CARRIAGELIKE: minus wheels.
52 JEEPLIKE: sometimes with a central turret.
53 BOOTEE-SHAPED: exceedingly rare.
54 HOUSE- OR HAYSTACK-SHAPED: apparently a roofed
boxlike UFO.
55 GENERATOR-SHAPED.
56 TRIGLOBULAR.
57 GRIDLIKE: can be square, round, closed, or open.
58 TWIN- OR MULTITAILED: body usually oval with two or
more tails.
59 IRREGULARLY SHAPED: objects of no known shape;
very rare.
60 S-SHAPED: has been observed in both the normal and re-
verse position.
61 HOOK-SHAPED: very rare.
62 DUMBBELL-SHAPED.
63 BIRD-SHAPED (not Mothman): usually gigantic body of a
general bird shape, with huge movable wings. (See
Fort, Wilkins, *et al.*, for reports.)

It is probable that further UFO types will be recognized as the record becomes more detailed and complete.

NOTE: The *UFO Register* is published by the Data Research Division of Contact (U.K.). The editor is Mr. J. B. Delair, and the address is 75 Norreys Road, Cumnor, near Oxford, OX2 9PU, England.

Appendix B.
Contact

The largest UFO movement in the world

The aims of Contact are to present the evidence for the presence of UFOs in our skies. Membership is open to all people of any color, race, or religion.

We have only had our technology for about two hundred years; but supposing that other planets in the galaxy had had theirs for thousands, maybe millions of years, then anything could be possible.

If you are interested in these ideas then you should join Contact. We live today on the threshold of great events; without any doubt at all the coming years will be the most exciting period in the history of mankind.

Brinsley Le Poer Trench
International Chairman

MEMBER COUNTRIES AND ADDRESSES OF
INTERNATIONAL COMMITTEE MEMBERS.

ARGENTINA
Professor Richard A. Frondizi
Hipolito Yrigoyen 3560. 8°. 24.
Buenos Aires

AUSTRALIA
Peter Burman, Esq.
Flat 7
111, Nelson Road
South Melbourne—3205
Victoria

BELGIUM
Comtesse R. d'Oultremont
Val des Pins
26, Dréve due Château
Linkebeek

CANADA
Mrs. Carol Halford-Watkins
95, Centre Street
Aylmer East
Quebec

CEYLON
Upali Amarasena
Amarani
Galboda
Induruwa

COLOMBIA
Albert Ron
Apartado Aereo 1320
Cali
Valle

CYPRUS
E.A.L. Coudounaris
P.O. Box 2405
Nicosia

FIJI ISLANDS
Yugeshwar Prakash
c/o Derrick Technical Institute
P.O. Box 3722
Samabula

ISRAEL
Amnon Yaish
Rehov Hapalmach 38
Jerusalem

ITALY
Dr. Alberto Perego
via Ruggero Fauro 43
Rome

MALAYSIA
Stephen T. S. Wong
Yulek Heights
T3, Lot 343, 5th Mile
Jalan Cheras
Kuala-Lumpur

MEXICO
Ing. I.C.M. Norrie
Benito Perez Galdos 218–201
Col. Polanco
Mexico 10
D.F.

NEW ZEALAND
Philip R. Austin
P.O. Box 10151
Balmoral
Auckland, 4

NIGERIA
Dr. O. E. Bogan
Box 19
Nwaniba via Uyo
South Eastern State

NORWAY
Nils Jacob Jacobsen
Disenveien, 111
Oslo, 5

PAKISTAN
Vill and P.O. Kazla
Kaligonj
Khulna
East Pakistan

PHILIPPINES
N.A. Villarruz
104, Roxas Avenue
Roxas City

PUERTO RICO
Noel E. Rigau
855, Las Marias Avenue
Rio Pedras
Puerto Rico—00927

RHODESIA
Mrs. Rhona T. Dippenaar
100, Percy Avenue
Hillside
Bulawayo

SOUTH AFRICA
John Elliot
P.O. Box 743
Durban
Natal

SPAIN
Miss Ruth Rees
Hotel Melia Torremolinos
Avenue Montemar
Torremolinos
Málaga

SWEDEN
Mrs. Edith C. M. Nicolaisen
Parthenon
Halsingborg, 5

SWITZERLAND
Leon Broch
13, rue de Bourg
1004, Lausanne

UNITED KINGDOM
F. W. Passey
59d Windmill Road
Headington
Oxford

UNITED STATES
Mrs. Madeline Teagle
548 Steeles Corners Road
Cuyahoga Falls
Ohio 44223

VENEZUELA
Andres Boulton Figueria de Mello
Apartado Postal 3623
Caracas

ZAMBIA
Donald G. MacLean
P.O. Box 1608
Ndola

Notes

1. John G. Fuller, "Flying Saucer Fiasco," *Look* magazine, May 14, 1968.
2. *Flying Saucer Review*, vol. 14, no. 3 (May-June, 1968). *FSR*, vol. 15, no. 2 (March-April, 1969), editorial. Charles H. Gibbs-Smith, "A Question of Integrity," *FSR*, vol. 16. no. 4 (July-August 1970) pp. 2–3. David R. Saunders and R. Roger Harkins, *UFOs? Yes! Where the Condon Committee Went Wrong*, Signet Books, New American Library, New York, 1968.
3. Dr. Edward U. Condon, *Scientific Study of Unidentified Flying Objects*, Bantam Books, New York, 1969.
4. Mrs. Judith M. Magee, "Mysterious Monuments on the Moon," *Australian Flying Saucer Review*, no. 2. (July 1970).
5. Harold T. Wilkins, *Flying Saucers on the Moon*, Peter Owen, London, 1954.
6. *Time* Magazine, July 27, 1962.
7. *Saga* magazine, date missing from cutting.
8. *Saga* magazine, May 1970.
9. Curtis Fuller, editorial, "I See by the Papers," *Fate* magazine, November 1970.
10. *Saga* magazine, May 1970.
11. Gordon W. Creighton, "Argentina 1962," *FSR*, vol. 10, no. 4 (July-August 1964), pp. 10–13.
12. Gordon W. Creighton, "Argentina 1963–64," in four parts, *FSR*, vol. 11, nos. 6–9 (November-December 1965, January-February, March-April, and May-June 1966), and "Further Reports of UFO Bases," vol. 15, no. 2 (March-April 1969).
13. Ivan T. Sanderson, *Invisible Residents*, World Publishing Company, Cleveland, Ohio. Published simultaneously in Canada by Nelson, Foster & Scott Ltd., 1970.
14. Edward J. Ruppelt, *The Report on Unidentified Flying Objects*, Doubleday & Company, Inc., Garden City, New York, 1956.

15. Dr. James McDonald, address to the American Society of Newspaper Editors in Washington, D.C., April 22, 1967.

16. Saunders and Harkins, *op. cit.,* p. 176.

17. B. Le Poer Trench, *The Sky People,* Wehman Brothers, Hackensack, New Jersey, 1961.

18. Captain Ivar Mackay, "UFOs and the Occult," *FSR,* vol. 16, no. 4 (July-August 1970) and vol. 16, no. 5 (September-October 1970).

19. Richard Tambling, *Flying Saucers—Where They Come From,* Scripts Pty. Ltd., London, Melbourne, Sydney, 1967.

20. Gordon W. Creighton, "Teleportations," *FSR,* vol. 11, no. 2 (March-April 1965).

21. *Ibid.* The following sources were quoted for the story about the Spanish soldier teleported from Manila to Mexico City: From *Las Calles de Mejico,* by Luis Gonzales Obregon, quoted in Part III of M. K. Jessup's *The Case for the UFO.* According to Jessup, further corroboration of the case is in the records of the chroniclers of the Order of San Augustín and the Order of Santo Domingo, and also in the book *Sucesos de las Islas Filipinas* (an account of Events in the Philippines) by Dr. Antonio de Morga, High Justice of the Criminal Court of the Royal Audiencia of New Spain.

22. Jacques Vallée, *Passport to Magonia,* Henry Regnery Company, Chicago, Illinois, 1969. pp. 98–99.

23. Aimé Michel, *Flying Saucers and the Straight-line Mystery,* Criterion Books, New York, 1958.

24. B. Le Poer Trench, *Operation Earth,* Wehman Brothers, Hackensack, New Jersey. pp. 49–52.

25. Gordon W. Creighton, "Teleportations," *FSR,* vol. 16, no. 5 (September-October, 1970).

26. Gordon W. Creighton, "More Teleportations," *FSR,* vol. 16, no. 5 (September-October, 1970).

27. John G. Fuller, *The Interrupted Journey,* Dial Press, New York, 1966. B. Le Poer Trench, *Operation Earth,* pp. 48–49. Worldwide press reports and articles.

28. Desmond Leslie and George Adamski, *Flying Saucers Have Landed,* British Book Center, Elmsford, New York, 1962.

29. *Encyclopaedia Britannica,* eleventh edition, vol 13.

30. Gordon W. Creighton, "The Humanoids in Latin America," from *The Humanoids,* edited by Charles Bowen, Henry Regnery Company, Chicago, Illinois, 1970.

31. *Ibid.,* pp. 111–13.

32. "World Round-up," *FSR,* vol. 16, no. 3 (May-June 1970). Sven-Olaf Fredrickson, "A Humanoid Was Seen at Imjärvi," *FSR,* vol. 16,

no. 5 (September-October 1970). "More on the Imjärvi Case," *FSR*, vol. 16, no. 6 (November-December 1970).

33. Anton Fitzgerald, "Repeat Performance," *FSR*, vol. 15, no. 3 (May-June 1969), originally published in the South African aviation magazine *Wings over Africa*.

34. Dr. Meade Layne, *The Coming of the Guardians*, privately printed, 1955.

35. "Mat and Demat," *FSR*, vol. 1, no. 4. (September-October 1955).

36. John A. Keel, *UFOs—Operation Trojan Horse*. G.P. Putnam's Sons, New York, 1970.

37. B. Le Poer Trench, *Operation Earth*, pp. 40–47.

38. Jacques and Janine Vallée, *Challenge to Science*. Henry Regnery Company, Chicago, Illinois, 1966.

39. B. Le Poer Trench, *Operation Earth*, pp. 74–75. Coral Lorenzen, "UFO Occupants in the United States," from *The Humanoids*, pp. 153–154.

40. Aimé Michel, *The Truth about Flying Saucers*, Criterion Books, New York, 1956.

41. Professor Charles A. Maney, "The Phenomena of Angel Hair," *FSR*, vol. 2, no. 6 (November-December 1956).

42. Gordon W. Creighton, "The Villa Santina Case," from *The Humanoids*, pp. 187–99.

43. Captain José Lemos Ferreira, "Air Force Pilots Spend Forty Minutes with Saucers," *FSR*, vol. 4, no. 3 (May-June 1958). B. Le Poer Trench, *The Flying Saucer Story*, Neville Spearman, London, 1966, pp. 41–44.

44. Gordon W. Creighton, "A New *FSR* Catalogue." Quoted from *FSR*, vol. 16, no. 1 (January-February 1970), no. 3 (May-June, 1970), no. 5 (September-October 1970), and no. 6 (November-December 1970). This book was completed before the series had finished, so there might well have been some more interesting cases to include, but I think I have made my point.

45. Louis Pauwels and Jacques Bergier, *The Morning of the Magicians*, Stein and Day, New York, New York, 1964. Originally published in France under the title *Le Matin des Magiciens*, by Editions Gallimard, Paris, 1960.

46. Garvin Gibbons, *The Coming of the Space Ships*, Neville Spearman, London, 1956.

47. Gordon W. Creighton, "The Humanoids in Latin America," from *The Humanoids*, p. 120.

48. *FSR*, vol. 3, no. 2 (March-April 1957), "Saucers over Midlands after Quakes," p. 2, and "World Round-up," p. 8.

49. *FSR*, vol. 10, no. 4 (July-August 1964), "The Deadly Bermuda Triangle." Author not named. Reprinted from February 1964 issue of *Argosy*.

50. B. Le Poer Trench, *Operation Earth*, pp. 63–64.

51. John A. Keel, *UFOs—Operation Trojan Horse*.

52. Ivan T. Sanderson, *Invisible Residents*. On the "Bermuda Triangle," pp. 115–42, and on "vile vortices," pp. 159–68.

53. Donald B. Hanlon, "The Airship . . . Fact and Fiction," *FSR*, vol. 16, no. 4 (July-August 1970).

54. Carl Grove, "The Airship Wave of 1909," *FSR*, vol. 16, no. 6 (November-December, 1970).

55. Henk J. Hinfelaar, "The New Zealand 'Flap' of 1909," *FSR*, vol. 10, no. 6 (November-December, 1964).

56. John A. Keel, "Mystery Aeroplanes of the 1930s," *FSR*, vol. 16, no. 3 (May-June 1970), and vol. 16, no. 4 (July-August 1970).

57. *Le Figaro*, September 5, 1946.

58. Bjorn Overbye, "Ghost-Bombs over Sweden," *FSR*, vol. 15, no. 2 (March-April 1969), and vol. 15, no. 3 (May-June 1969).

59. Richard Hall, editor, *The UFO Evidence*, published by the National Investigations Committee on Aerial Phenomena (NICAP), Washington, D.C., 1964.

60. Manly Palmer Hall, *The Most Holy Trinosophia of the Comte de St.-Germain*. Philosophers Press, Los Angeles, 1949.

61. *Encyclopaedia Britannica*, eleventh edition.

62. *Contact (U.S.A.)* magazine, April 1970.

63. Antonio Ribera, "The San José de Valderas Photographs," *FSR*, vol. 15, no. 5 (September-October 1969), and an earlier article, "The Madrid Landing," *FSR*, vol. 12, no. 3 (May-June 1966).

64. W. T. Powers, "The Landing at Socorro," from *The Humanoids*, pp. 130–42.

65. Derek D. Dempster, "Let's Talk Space," *FSR*, vol. 2, no. 1 (January-February, 1956).

66. E. Frederick Schrafft (as told to Paul Braczyk), "Project Doomsday: The UFO," *Flying Saucers*, published in Amherst, Wisconsin, issue no. 72, March 1971.

67. Antonio Ribera, letter to the author.

68. E. A. Wallis Budge, translator, *The Book of the Dead*, Papyrus of Ani in the British Museum, Dover Publications, Inc., 1967.

69. *The Popul-Vuh*. The Sacred Book of the Quiché-Maya. English version by Delia Goetz and Sylvanus G. Morley from the Spanish translation by Adrian Recinos. University of Oklahoma Press, Norman, Oklahoma, 1969.

70. Lama Anagarika Govinda, *Foundations of Tibetan Mysticism*, Samuel Weiser, New York, New York, 1970.

71. Noah Kramer, *From the Tablets of Sumer*, Falcon's Wing Press, Indian Hills, Colorado, 1956.

72. Erich von Daniken, *Return to the Stars*, G. P. Putnam's Sons, New York, New York, 1971. pp. 39–41.

73. Otto O. Binder, *Flying Saucers Are Watching Us*, Belmont Books, New York, 1968.

74. I. S. Shklovskii and Carl Sagan, *Intelligent Life in the Universe*, Holden-Day, San Francisco, 1966.

75. Fred Hoyle, *Of Men and Galaxies*, University of Washington Press, Seattle, Washington, 1966.

76. Gordon W. Creighton, "The Most Amazing Case of All," *FSR*, vol. 11, no. 1 (January-February 1965), no. 2 (March-April 1965), no. 4 (July-August 1965). "Even More Amazing," vol. 12, no. 4 (July-August 1966), no. 5 (September-October 1966), no. 6 (November-December 1966), vol. 13, no. 1 (January-February 1967). "The Amazing Case of Antonio Villas Boas," from *The Humanoids*, hardcover edition (not in original paperback special issue by *FSR*), pp. 200–38. Dr. Olavo Fontes, "Even More Amazing," part 5. Dr. Fontes, who regrettably died May 9, 1968, contributed the last article of the series. *FSR*, vol. 13, no. 3 (May-June 1967).

77. Ben Barzman, *Out of This World*, Collins, London, 1960, pp. 261–62.

78. Fulcanelli, *Le Mystère des Cathédrales*, translated from the French by Mary Sworder, Neville Spearman, London, 1971.

79. London *Daily Telegraph* color magazines, April 30, May 7 and 14, 1971.

80. Jonathan Swift, *Gulliver's Travels*, 1726.

81. Charles Fort, *The Books of Charles Fort*, published for the Fortean Society by Henry Holt and Company, New York, 1941.

82. Erich von Daniken, *Chariots of the Gods* and *Return to the Stars*, G. P. Putnam's Sons, New York, New York, 1970 and 1971 respectively.

83. Joseph Millard, *Edgar Cayce—Man of Miracles*, Wehman Brothers, Hackensack, New Jersey, 1963. Jess Stearn, *Edgar Cayce—The Sleeping Prophet*, Doubleday & Company, Inc., Garden City, New York, 1967.

84. Dr. Immanuel Velikovsky, *Worlds in Collision*, Macmillan, 1950. Subsequently republished by Doubleday & Company, Inc. Incidentally, as a matter of academic interest, this book had over three thousand reviews and probably created the biggest controversy in literary history.

Index

Abraham, angels and, 33
Adam, 144–45
Air Forces, 16, 27–28, 75–76
Airplanes, "phantom," 103–6, 110, 113
Airships, 97–102, 110, 112–13
Aldrin, Buzz, 20
Alexander the Great, 77
Alora, Horacio, 24
Angel hair, 70–72
Animals, 77–84; and Creation, 145–46; and weightlessness, 61ff.
Apollo missions, 20–21
Appleton, Cynthia, 67
Argentina, 22–25, 55, 60
Armstrong, Neil, 20
Asimov, Isaac, 169
Astronauts, 19–21
Atomic bomb, 15–16
Australia, 81

Barzman, Ben, 160
Bean, Allan, 21
Bearland, G., 99
Bergier, Jacques, 85–86, 157ff.
"Bermuda Triangle," 90, 91
Berry, Adrian, 167, 174
Besutti, José, 24
Bible, 15, 33–39, 52; Genesis, 33, 140ff., 144, 145, 149, 150
Binder, Otto O., 148–49
Blue Book, Project, 27–29
Bordoli, Vicente A., 25

Boutlerow, Professor von, 59
Boville, Miss H. M., 98–99
Brain, 148–52. See also Intelligence
Brazil, 56
Brew, Charles, 81
Britain and the British (England; United Kingdom), 15, 81–82, 87, 89, 91; airships over, 98–100, 113; and cloud UFOs, 52–53, 54

Cansiliet, Eugène, 164
Catholic Church, 59
Cayce, Edgar, 173
Central Intelligence Agency (CIA), 28–30, 122
Challenge to Science, 67–68
Children, new race of, 157–62
"Cigars." See Airships; Clouds; Rockets
Clouds, 52–57
Colorado, University of, 16
Coming of the Guardians, The, 65
Condon, Dr. Edward U., 16
Condon Report, 16–17, 28
Conrad, Pete, 21
Contact, 115ff., 181–83
Cooper, Gordon, 19–20
Cosmology, 135–53
Creighton, Gordon W., 22–24, 25, 50–52, 55, 60, 73, 74, 77ff.
Cro-Magnon Man, 159
Crookes, Sir William, 59

Danielli, Dr. James, 153
Daniken, Erich von, 144, 172
Darbishire, Stephen, 87
Darwin, Charles, 148
Day, A. V., 99
Deimos, 169
Dempster, Derek D., 123–24
Denmark, 105
"Devil's Triangle," 90, 91
Dewilde, Marius, 79

Earthquakes, 89, 90
Ectoplasm, 69ff.
Egenes, Captain, 99
Egypt, 140
Einstein, Albert, 167
Elijah, 35
Elisha, 35–36
Elohim, 138, 139, 142–43, 145
Emblem, UFO, 120–24
Enders, Robert K., 158–59
England. See Britain and the British
Enoch, 35
Expansion and contraction, 73–76
Ezekiel, 34–35

Faceless woman, 114–19
Ferraz, Marcilo, 56
Finland, 60–61, 108
Fitzgerald, Anton, 61–63
Flindt, Max H., 148, 151
Flying Saucer Review. See specific
    subjects, writers
Flying Saucer Story, The, 122
Flying Saucers—Where They Come
    From, 50
Fontes, Dr. Olavo, 151
Fort, Charles, 171
France, 53, 67–68, 70–71, 78–79
Fulcanelli (alchemist), 164
Fuller, John G., 57, 82

Garden of Eden, 145
Gate of the Sun, 90–91
Ghana, 79–80
God, 133, 137ff., 144ff., 165
Gómez Pérez Dasmarinas, Don,
    51
Gordon, Dick, 21
Graeffer, Franz, 111

Gravity, 123–24, 132
Grove, Carl, 98–100
Gulliver's Travels, 169

Hanlon, Donald B., 87, 97–98
Hansen, Dollie, 115–16
Harkins, R. Rogers, 28–29
Harranians, 142
Harvey, Luis, 23
Hearing, 83–84
Heim, Dr. Burkhard, 123
Heinonen, Aarno, 60–61
Henderson, Dr. Garry, 20
Henry, Lt., 109
Hill, Mr. and Mrs. Barney, 57–58,
    80–81
Hindu Vedas, 15
Hinfelaar, Henk J., 100–2
Home, Daniel Dunglas, 59
Howard, Captain, 74
Hoyle, Fred, 150
Humanity, manufacture of, 144–47
Humanoids, 118–19
Humanoids, The, 73–75
Hynek, Dr. J. Allen, 122
Hyperspace, 167ff.

Incident at Exeter, 82
Intelligence (I.Q.), 157ff. See also
    Brain
Intelligent Life in the Universe,
    149–50
Interbreeding, 148–52
Interrupted Journey, The, 57
Invisible Residents, 26, 91
Israelites. See Bible
Italy, 73–74

Jacob, 36
Japan, 55–56
Jehovah, 139, 145
Jericho, Walls of, 33
Jesus, 36–38
Johannis, Rapuzzi Luigi, 73–74
Jordan, Dr. Pascual, 123

Kazantzev, M., 91
Kearney, Neb., 90

Keel, John A., 66–67, 68, 90, 94, 161;
  on mystery airplanes, 103–5
Kinoshita, Mr., 55, 56

Lake Titicaca, 25
Lattice, the, 163–65
Layne, Dr. Meade, 65–66
Lemos Ferreira, José, 75–76
Leslie, Desmond, 59
Leslie, Ted, 63
Levitation, 59–64
Lot, 33
Low, Robert J., 16–17

McDonald, Dr. James E., 28, 81
Mackay, Ivar, 49, 59, 69, 73, 185
Magee, Judith M., 19
Magnetic deviation, 89
Maney, Charles A., 71
Martin Aircraft Company, 123
Martinez, Felipe, 60
Marys, the Three, 37–38
Materializations, 65–68
Maya. See Quiché-Maya
Mental pictures, 94
Mexico, 50–52, 56–57
Michel, Aimé, 53, 54, 70–71, 78–79
Moon, 18–21
Morning of the Magicians, 85–86,
  157ff.
Moses, 33–34
Muñoz, Antonio, 121
Muscarello case, 82
Mutants, 157–62
Mystère des Cathédrales, Le, 164

NASA, 122, 123
Nature of Living Things, The, 158–59
Nautilus, U.S.S., 86
New Mexico, 122, 123
New York City, mystery planes over,
  103, 104
New Zealand, 15, 100–2, 113
Norway, 105

Of Men and Galaxies, 150
Ohio, 114–18
Oily substances, 69
On Tiptoe Beyond Darwin, 148

O'Neill, John J., 19
Operation Earth, 97, 166, 167
Orbiter-2, 18–19
Out of This World, 160
Overbye, Bjorn, 107–8

Palmer, Ray, 124
Passport to Magonia, 52, 83
Paul, St., 36
Pauwels, Louis, 85–86, 157ff.
Peru, 87, 90
Peter, St., 38–39
Phobus, 169
Popul-Vuh, the, 140–42, 145, 146–47
Portugal, 75–76
Precipitations, 69–72
Pressey, Dr. Sydney, 159
Psychic phenomena, 47–94
Puckett, Jack E., 109

Quiché-Maya, 140–42, 145, 146–47

Rabot, M., 53
Radar, 170
Rand Corporation, 85–86
Ravenna, Ohio, 90
Recollections of Vienna, 111
Relativity, theory of, 167
Religion. See Bible; Cosmology;
  Saints
Report on Unidentified Flying Objects,
  The, 27
Return to the Stars, 144
Reutersward, Major General, 105
Rhine, Dr. J. B., 85
Ribera, Antonio, 120–21, 122, 124
Riedel, Dr. Walter, 21
Robertson Committee, 29
Rockets, mystery, 107–9, 110, 113
Rugel, Jake, 62–63
Ruppelt, Edward J., 27
Russia, 85, 86

Saga, 20–21
Sagan, Dr. Carl, 21, 149–50, 174
St.-Germain, Comte de, 111
Saints, 59
San Andreas fault, 90
Sanderson, Ivan T., 26, 91, 168–69

Saunders, David R., 28–29
Scandinavia, 16, 104–5; ghost rockets
    seen in, 107–9, 113
Schmidt, Reinhold, 69
Shklovskii, Dr. I. S., 149
Simons, Dr. Benjamin, 58
Size, 73–76, 131–32
Sky People, The, 138–39
Smith, Wilbert B., 88
Soal, Dr. J. S., 85
Socorro, New Mexico, 122, 123
Sodom, 33
South Africa, 61–62, 81
South America, 22–26. *See also*
    specific countries
Space, 167–69
Spain, 120–22ff.
Star of Bethlehem, 36–37
Steam engines, 111–12
Stephenson, George, 112
Strontium, 90, 157, 158, 161
Submarines, 85–86
Sumerians, 142, 149–50
Superspace, 167–69, 172ff.
Sweden, 104, 105, 107
Swift, Jonathan, 169
Symington, William, 112

Tambling, R., 50
Teagle, Madeline, 115ff.
Telekinesis, 93–94
Telepathy, 85–88
Teleportation, 50–58
Television (TV) interference, 115
Teresa of Avila, St., 59
Terman, Lewis, 159
Texas, 62–63
Tiahuanaca, 90–91
Tibetans, 142
Trains, 111, 112
Truth about Flying Saucers, The. See
    Michel, Aimé

United States. *See* specific incidents,
    persons, places
UFOs—Operation Trojan Horse,
    66–67, 94
UFOs? Yes!, 28–29

Vallée, Jacques, 52, 67–68, 83
Vallée, Janine, 67–68
Vedas, 15
Velikovsky, Dr. Immanuel, 174
Vellacca, Joyce, 117–18
Venezuela, 60, 90, 91
Venus, 174
Vidal, Dr. and Mrs. Gerardo, 55
"Vile vortices," 91–92, 168–69
Viljo, Esko, 60–61
Villas-Boas, Antonio, 151
Villa Santina case, 73–74

Wanaque, N. J., 90
War of the Worlds, 30
Weightlessness, 61–64
Welles, Orson, 30
Wells, H. G., 30
Wheeler, John A., 167, 168, 171,
    172ff.
Whidby Island, 74
White, Robert, 19
Wilde, J. O. S., 79–80
Wilkins, Dr. H. P., 19
"Windows," 89–92
World War I, 52–53
Worlds in Collision, 174
Worth, C. Brooke, 158–59
Wright brothers, 100

Zamora, Lonnie, 122
Zeppelin, Count Ferdinand von, 97,
    100